Elspeth Barker was born in Scotland and educated there and at Oxford. Her novel *O Caledonia* was widely acclaimed. She is the widow of the poet George Barker. She has five children and now lives in Norfolk.

LOSS

EDITED BY

Elspeth Barker

ORION

An Orion Paperback
First published in Great Britain by J. M. Dent in 1997
This paperback edition published in 1998 by
Orion Books Ltd,
Orion House, 5 Upper St Martin's Lane
London WC2H 9EA

A CIP catalogue record for this book
is available from the British Library.

ISBN 0 75281 670 5

Typeset at The Spartan Press Ltd,
Lymington, Hants
Printed and bound in Great Britain by
Clays Ltd, St Ives plc

CONTENTS

INTRODUCTION

As my guide and mentor in assembling this volume I have
used Wordsworth's:

> Fallings from us, vanishings;
> Blank misgivings of a creature
> Moving about in worlds not realised.

The knowledge and experience of loss has so wide a span,
ranging from the exquisite poignancy of a changing season
to the desolation of bereavement. The infant Colette's
startled recognition of something pagan and unpredictable
in her mother, or David Wright's realization that he is deaf,
also have their place in this spectrum.

Initially I collected three times as much material as was
permitted and suffered greatly through the process of
elimination. My editor suffered even more. Many poems
were too long to be included and were not susceptible to
cutting. Among these were Milton's *Lycidas*, William Dun-
bar's 'Lament for the Makers' and the anonymous *Quia
Amore Langueo*. Some poets have written almost exclusively
about loss and it was hard to select from their work. I
hoarded great quantities of Emily Dickinson, A.E. Housman, Stevie Smith, Larkin, Tennyson and, of course, Shake-
speare, who is an inexhaustible source on this subject as on
everything else.

I have included only a handful of poems on war as there
are many excellent anthologies of war poetry available. I
have used few translations, partly on grounds of literary

merit, but chiefly in view of the overwhelming wealth of material written in English. Thus several all-time towering geniuses have been excluded: Homer, Virgil and Catullus for a start. I was also surprised to discover how few prose passages could be effectively isolated from their context. In contrast, poetry spoke directly. In a letter to his sister, whose son had been killed in Flanders, A.E. Housman wrote: 'It is the function of poetry to harmonise the sadness of the world.' There can be no consolation but there may be comfort, in the old sense of drawing strength, as in the wonderful passage 'Comfort ye, my people' in Handel's Messiah: the knowledge of universality. The need for this form of communion, and its power, were overwhelmingly apparent at the recent funeral of Diana, Princess of Wales.

I did not wish to arrange these extracts according to theme. I feel that here this would be degrading to passion and to content and would run the risk of creating a sort of doomy Disneyland featuring Dead Dogs' Corner, Amputees' Grotto, and so on.

Finally, I hope that this volume, despite its sombre nature, may be read as a celebration of what has been, of the value of our laborious days. George Crabbe's modest, beautiful poem on his late wife's wedding ring says it all in four lines.

ANONYMOUS

Western Wind

Western wind, when wilt thou blow
That the small rain down can rain.
Christ, that my love were in my arms,
And I in my bed again.

ELIZABETH BISHOP

One Art

The art of losing isn't hard to master;
so many things seem filled with the intent
to be lost that their loss is no disaster.

Lose something every day. Accept the fluster
of lost door keys, the hour badly spent.
The art of losing isn't hard to master.

Then practice losing farther, losing faster:
places, and names, and where it was you meant
to travel. None of these will bring disaster.

I lost my mother's watch. And look! my last, or
next-to-last, of three loved houses went.
The art of losing isn't hard to master.

I lost two cities, lovely ones. And, vaster,
some realms I owned, two rivers, a continent.
I miss them, but it wasn't a disaster.

– Even losing you (the joking voice, a gesture
I love) I shan't have lied. It's evident
the art of losing's not too hard to master
though it may look like (*Write* it!) like disaster.

GEORGE BARKER

Never, My Love and Dearest

Never, my love and dearest,
　　we'll hear the lilies grow
or, silent and dancing,
　　the fall of the winter snow,
or the great clouds of Summer
　　as on their way they go.

Never, my love and dearest,
　　we'll hear the bluebells chime
or the whole world turn over
　　after the harvest time.
O not everything, my dearest,
　　needs to be said in rhyme!

WILLIAM EMPSON

Missing Dates

Slowly the poison the whole blood stream fills.
It is not the effort nor the failure tires.
The waste remains, the waste remains and kills.

It is not your system or clear sight that mills
Down small to the consequence a life requires;
Slowly the poison the whole blood stream fills.

They bled an old dog dry yet the exchange rills
Of young dog blood gave but a month's desires
The waste remains, the waste remains and kills.

It is the Chinese tombs and the slag hills
Usurp the soil, and not the soil retires.
Slowly the poison the whole blood stream fills.

Not to have fire is to be a skin that shrills.
The complete fire is death. From partial fires
The waste remains, the waste remains and kills.

It is the poems you have lost, the ills
From missing dates, at which the heart expires.
Slowly the poison the whole blood stream fills.
The waste remains, the waste remains and kills.

LORD BYRON

'So, we'll go no more a-roving'

So, we'll go no more a-roving
    So late into the night,
Though the heart be still as loving,
    And the moon be still as bright.

For the sword outwears its sheath,
    And the soul outwears the breast,
And the heart must pause to breathe,
    And love itself have rest.

Though the night was made for loving,
    And the day returns too soon,
Yet we'll go no more a-roving
    By the light of the moon.

ANONYMOUS

The Twa Corbies

As I was walking all alane,
I heard twa corbies making a mane: *crows*
The tane unto the tither did say,
'Whar sall we gang and dine the day?'

'– In ahint yon auld fail dyke *turf*
I wot there lies a new-slain knight;
And naebody kens that he lies there
But his hawk, his hound, and his lady fair.

'His hound is to the hunting gane,
His hawk to fetch the wild-fowl hame,
His lady's ta'en anither mate,
So we may mak' our dinner sweet.

'Ye'll sit on his white hause-bane, *collar bone*
And I'll pike out his bonny blue e'en:
Wi' ae lock o' his gowden hair
We'll theek our nest when it grows bare. *thatch*

'Mony a one for him maks mane,
But nane sall ken whar he is gane:
O'er his white banes, when they are bare,
The wind sall blaw for evermair.'

ROBERT GRAVES

Lost Love

His eyes are quickened so with grief,
He can watch a grass or leaf
Every instant grow; he can
Clearly through a flint wall see,
Or watch the startled spirit flee
From the throat of a dead man.
    Across two counties he can hear
And catch your words before you speak.
The woodlouse or the maggot's weak
Clamour rings in his sad ear;
And noise so slight it would surpass
Credence: – drinking sound of grass,
Worm talk, clashing jaws of moth
Chumbling holes in cloth:
The groan of ants who undertake
Gigantic loads for honour's sake,
Their sinews creak, their breath comes thin;
Whir of spiders when they spin,
And minute whispering, mumbling, sighs
Of idle grubs and flies.
    This man is quickened so with grief,
He wanders god-like or like thief
Inside and out, below, above,
Without relief seeking lost love.

VLADIMIR NABOKOV

A Moth (from *Speak, Memory*)

When, having shaken off all pursuers, I took the rough, red
road that ran from our house toward field and forest, the
animation and lustre of the day seemed like a tremor of
sympathy around me. Black *Erebia* butterflies ('Ringlets' as
the old English Aurelians used to call them), with a special
gentle awkwardness peculiar to their kind, danced among
the firs. From a flower head two male Coppers rose to a
tremendous height, fighting all the way up – and then, after
a while came the downward flash of one of them returning
to his thistle. These were familiar insects, but at any
moment something better might cause me to stop with a
quick intake of breath. I remember one day when I warily
brought my net closer and closer to a little *Thecla* that had
daintily settled on a sprig. I could clearly see the white *W* on
its chocolate-brown underside. Its wings were closed and
the inferior ones were rubbing against each other in a
curious circular motion – possibly producing some small,
blithe crepitation pitched too high for a human ear to catch.
I had long wanted that particular species, and, when near
enough, I struck. You have heard champion tennis players
moan after muffing an easy shot. You have seen stunned
golfers smile horrible, helpless smiles. But that day nobody
saw me shake out a piece of twig from an otherwise empty
net and stare at a hole in the tarlatan.

MATTHEW ARNOLD

Dover Beach

The sea is calm tonight.
The tide is full, the moon lies fair
Upon the straits; on the French coast the light
Gleams and is gone; the cliffs of England stand,
Glimmering and vast, out in the tranquil bay.
Come to the window, sweet is the night-air!
Only, from the long line of spray
Where the sea meets the moon-blanched land,
Listen! you hear the grating roar
Of pebbles which the waves draw back, and fling,
At their return, up the high strand,
Begin, and cease, and then again begin,
With tremulous cadence slow, and bring
The eternal note of sadness in.

Sophocles long ago
Heard it on the Aegean, and it brought
Into his mind the turbid ebb and flow
Of human misery; we
Find also in the sound a thought,
Hearing it by this distant northern sea.

The Sea of Faith
Was once, too, at the full, and round earth's shore
Lay like the folds of a bright girdle furled.

But now I only hear
Its melancholy, long, withdrawing roar,
Retreating, to the breath
Of the night-wind, down the vast edges drear
And naked shingles of the world.

Ah, love, let us be true
To one another! for the world, which seems
To lie before us like a land of dreams,
So various, so beautiful, so new,
Hath really neither joy, nor love, nor light,
Nor certitude, nor peace, nor help for pain;
And we are here as on a darkling plain
Swept with confused alarms of struggle and flight,
Where ignorant armies clash by night.

Remember Now Thy Creator
(Ecclesiastes 12:1–8)

Remember now thy Creator in the days of thy youth, while the evil days come not, nor the years draw nigh, when thou shalt say, I have no pleasure in them;

While the sun, or the light, or the moon, or the stars, be not darkened, nor the clouds return after the rain:

In the day when the keepers of the house shall tremble, and the strong men shall bow themselves, and the grinders cease because they are few, and those that look out of the windows be darkened.

And the doors shall be shut in the streets, when the sound of the grinding is low, and he shall rise up at the voice of the bird, and all the daughters of music shall be brought low;

Also *when* they shall be afraid of *that which is* high, and fears *shall be* in the way and the almond tree shall flourish, and the grasshopper shall be a burden, and desire shall fail: because man goeth to his long home, and the mourners go about the streets:

Or ever the silver cord be loosed, or the golden bowl be broken, or the pitcher be broken at the fountain, or the wheel broken at the cistern.

Then shall the dust return to the earth as it was: and the spirit shall return unto God who gave it.

Vanity of vanities, saith the preacher; all *is* vanity.

SARAH THOMAS

Taking Your Problems With You

We have to go, me and you.
It isn't being kind
my son said. He knew
his dad would mind.

It isn't being kind
escaping this place.
His dad would mind.
I'm bruised everywhere but my face.

Escaping this place –
We have to go, me and you.
I'm bruised everywhere but my face.
My son said he knew.

EMILY DICKINSON

Softened By Time

Softened by Time's consummate plush,
　　How sleek the woe appears
That threatened childhood's citadel
　　And undermined the years!

Bisected now by bleaker griefs,
　　We envy the despair
That threatened childhood's citadel
　　So easy to repair.

W.B. YEATS

from 'A Man Young and Old'

Like the moon her kindness is,
If kindness I may call
What has no comprehension in't,
But is the same for all
As though my sorrow were a scene
Upon a painted wall.

So like a bit of stone I lie
Under a broken tree.
I could recover if I shrieked
My heart's agony
To passing bird, but I am dumb
From human dignity.

ALFRED, LORD TENNYSON

Tears, Idle Tears (from *The Princess*)

Tears, idle tears, I know not what they mean,
Tears from the depth of some divine despair
Rise in the heart, and gather to the eyes,
In looking on the happy autumn-fields,
And thinking of the days that are no more.

Fresh as the first beam glittering on a sail,
That brings our friends up from the underworld,
Sad as the last which reddens over one
That sinks with all we love below the verge;
So sad, so fresh, the days that are no more.

Ah, sad and strange as in dark summer dawns
The earliest pipe of half-awakened birds
To dying ears, when unto dying eyes
The casement slowly grows a glimmering square;
So sad, so strange, the days that are no more.

Dear as remembered kisses after death,
And sweet as those by hopeless fancy feigned
On lips that are for others; deep as love,
Deep as first love, and wild with all regret;
O Death in Life, the days that are no more.

GEOFFREY GODBERT

The Politics of Exile

There is no language left for them;
only silence like hunger,
sight without focus, insomnia.
Seated, they breathe as if running;
see mirages behind them;
walk on crutches, feed on pills.
They are offered life without rest.

They can always go somewhere else
(but never home again).
They can always fall in love
(but not with their sweetheart).
They can always be adopted
(but not by their flesh and blood).

They are not encouraged to dream,
but there is nothing to stop them
aspiring to be someone new,
because they had never existed;
otherwise, they would have
to remain who they really are,
which no one, by now, can remember.

If they continue to mutter
regrets to themselves,

then there is no option
other than to commit them,
out of harm's way, for their own good;
for everyone's peace of mind,
someone has to put them somewhere
as solitary as themselves,
to work out their own way of death.

But if they once acknowledge
the streets outside are paved with gold
and this land is made of milk and honey,
then, of course, they will benefit:
they could be let loose, free as birds.

RAINER MARIA RILKE

from *Duino Elegies*

Who, if I cried, would hear me among the angelic
orders? And even if one of them suddenly
pressed me against his heart, I should fade in the strength
  of his
stronger existence. For Beauty's nothing
but beginning of Terror we're still just able to bear,
and why we adore it so is because it serenely
disdains to destroy us. Each single angel is terrible.
And so I repress myself, and swallow the call-note
of depth-dark sobbing. Alas, who is there
we can make use of? Not angels, not men;
and already the knowing brutes are aware
that we don't feel very securely at home
within our interpreted world.

JOHN CLARE

I Am

I am – yet what I am none cares or knows,
   My friends forsake me like a memory lost;
I am the self-consumer of my woes,
   They rise and vanish in oblivions host,
Like shadows in love – frenzied stifled throes
And yet I am, and live like vapours tost

Into the nothingness of scorn and noise,
   Into the living sea of waking dreams,
Where there is neither sense of life or joys,
   But the vast shipwreck of my life's esteems;
And e'en the dearest – that I love the best –
Are strange – nay, rather stranger than the rest.

I long for scenes where man has never trod,
   A place where woman never smiled or wept;
There to abide with my Creator, God,
   And sleep as I in childhood sweetly slept;
Untroubling and untroubled where I lie,
The grass below – above the vaulted sky.

A.E. HOUSMAN

Diffugere Nives
(Horace, Odes, iv, 7)

The snows are fled away, leaves on the shaws
    And grasses in the mead renew their birth,
The river to the river-bed withdraws,
    And altered is the fashion of the earth.

The Nymphs and Graces three put off their fear
    And unapparelled in the woodland play.
The swift hour and the brief prime of the year
    Say to the soul, *Thou wast not born for aye.*

Thaw follows frost; hard on the heel of spring
    Treads summer sure to die, for hard on hers
Comes autumn with his apples scattering;
    Then back to wintertide, when nothing stirs.

But oh, whate'er the sky-led seasons mar,
    Moon upon moon rebuilds it with her beams;
Come we where Tullus and where Ancus are
    And good Aeneas, we are dust and dreams.

Torquatus, if the gods in heaven shall add
    The morrow to the day, what tongue has told?
Feast then thy heart, for what thy heart has had
    The fingers of no heir will ever hold.

When thou descendest once the shades among,
    The stern assize and equal judgment o'er,
Not thy long lineage nor thy golden tongue,
    No, nor thy righteousness, shall friend thee more.

Night holds Hippolytus the pure of stain,
    Diana steads him nothing, he must stay;
And Theseus leaves Pirithous in the chain
    The love of comrades cannot take away.

ANNA AKHMATOVA

from *Prison Poems*

Already madness has covered
half my soul with its wing,
and gives me strong liquor to drink,
and lures me to the black valley.

I realised that I must
hand victory to it,
as I listened to my delirium,
already alien to me.

It will not allow me to take
anything away with me
(however I beseech it,
however I pester it with prayer):

not the terrible eyes of my son,
the rock-like suffering,
not the day when the storm came,
not the prison visiting hour,

nor the sweet coolness of hands,
nor the uproar of the lime trees' shadows,
nor the distant, light sound –
the comfort of last words.

D.H. LAWRENCE

Piano

Softly, in the dusk, a woman is singing to me;
Taking me back down the vista of years, till I see
A child sitting under the piano, in the boom of the tingling
    strings
And pressing the small, poised feet of a mother who smiles
    as she sings.

In spite of myself, the insidious mastery of song
Betrays me back, till the heart of me weeps to belong
To the old Sunday evenings at home, with winter outside
And hymns in the cosy parlour, the tinkling piano our
    guide.

So now it is vain for the singer to burst into clamour
With the great black piano appassionato. The glamour
Of childish days is upon me, my manhood is cast
Down in the flood of remembrance, I weep like a child for
    the past.

CHARLES LAMB

The Old Familiar Faces

I have had playmates, I have had companions,
In my days of childhood, in my joyful school-days,
All, all are gone, the old familiar faces.

I have been laughing, I have been carousing,
Drinking late, sitting late, with my bosom cronies,
All, all are gone, the old familiar faces.

I loved a love once, fairest among women:
Closed are her doors on me, I must not see her –
All, all are gone, the old familiar faces.

I have a friend, a kinder friend has no man;
Like an ingrate, I left my friend abruptly;
Left him, to muse on the old familiar faces.

Ghost-like I paced round the haunts of my childhood,
Earth seemed a desert I was bound to traverse,
Seeking to find the old familiar faces.

Friend of my bosom, thou more than a brother,
Why wert not thou born in my father's dwelling?
So might we talk of the old familiar faces –

How some they have died, and some they have left me,
And some are taken from me; all are departed;
All, all are gone, the old familiar faces.

OVID

Exile

Since I have been in Pontus, the Danube has frozen over three times, and three times the water of the Euxine has hardened with the cold. But I feel as if I were as many years away from my country as Dardanian Troy was invested by her Greek enemy. You would think the seasons stood still, so slowly do they advance and with lagging steps does the year accomplish its journey. For me the summer solstice takes nothing from the nights nor for me does the winter shorten the days. Doubtless in myself the nature of things has been changed, and makes everything as protracted as my woes. Or do the usual seasons run their wonted courses, and is it rather this cruel season of my life that is standing still? Here I am confined by the shore of the falsely named Euxine and the land of the Scythian sea, sinister indeed.

Around me countless tribes threaten savage war, and think it disgraceful not to live on plunder. Nothing is safe outside: the hill itself is defended by meagre walls and the nature of the site. When you least expect it, like birds the swarming enemy dart in and drive off their booty almost before they have been seen. Often in the middle of the streets we pick up their deadly arrows that come dropping inside the walls when the gates have been shut. Rare, therefore, is the man who dares to till the fields; he ploughs unhappily with one hand and holds his arms in the other. Under a helmet the shepherd plays on his pitch-bound reeds and instead of the wolf it is wars of which the timorous sheep are afraid. Hardly are we defended by the help of the fort; and even inside, the crowd of barbarians mingled with Greeks causes consternation. Indeed the barbarian lives among us with no distinction, and, what is more, occupies more than half of the buildings. Even if you did not fear them, you could loathe them when you saw their chests covered with skins and long hair.

Even those who are thought to originate from the Greek city wear Persian trousers instead of their native dress. They use a common tongue for communication: I have to explain things by gestures. Here I am the barbarian, who am understood by no one, and the stupid Getae laugh at my Latin words. Often before my face they safely speak ill of me, and perhaps they are taunting me with my banishment. As often happens, if they are speaking, whenever I nod dissent or assent, they think there is some deceit in me. Besides, justice that is no justice is dispensed with the harsh sword, and often wounds are inflicted in the middle of the forum. O cruel Lachesis, who to one with a star so burdensome gave not a shorter thread of life! It is because I cannot see my country's face or yours, my friends, and because I am here among the tribes of Scythia, that I complain: each is a heavy penalty. Though I deserved to leave the city, I did not deserve, perhaps, to be in such a place. O fool, what am I saying? For offending Caesar's majesty, I deserved to lose my very life as well.

A.E. HOUSMAN

We'll to the Woods No More

We'll to the woods no more,
The laurels all are cut,
The bowers are bare of bay
That once the Muses wore;
The year draws in the day
And soon will evening shut:
The laurels all are cut,
We'll to the woods no more.
Oh we'll no more, no more
To the leafy woods away,
To the high wild woods of laurel
And the bowers of bay no more.

DAVID GRAY

from *In The Shadows*

Last night, on coughing slightly with sharp pain,
    There came arterial blood, and with a sigh
Of absolute grief I cried in bitter vein,
    That drop is my death warrant: I must die.
Poor meagre life is mine, meagre and poor!
    Rather a piece of childhood thrown away;
An adumbration faint; the overture
    To stifled music; year that ends in May;
The sweet beginning of a tale unknown;
    A dream unspoken; promise unfulfilled;
A morning with no noon, a rose unblown –
    All is deep rich vermilion crushed and killed
I' th' bud by frost – Thus in false fear I cried,
Forgetting to abolish death Christ died.

Hew Atlas for my monument; upraise
    A pyramid for my tomb, that, undestroyed
    By rank, oblivion, and the hungry void,
My name shall echo through prospective days.
    O careless conqueror! cold, abysmal grave!
Is it not sad – is it not sad, my heart –
To smother young ambition, and depart
    Unhonoured and unwilling, like death's slave?
No rare immortal remnant of my thought
    Embalms my life; no poem, firmly reared

Against the shock of time, ignobly feared –
But all my life's progression come to nought.
Hew Atlas! build a pyramid in a plain!
Oh, cool the fever burning in my brain!

Wise in his day that heathen emperor,
    To whom, each morrow, came a slave, and cried –
'Philip, remember thou must die': no more.
    To me such daily voice were misapplied –
Disease guests with me; and each cough, or cramp,
    Or aching, like the Macedonian slave,
Is my *memento mori*. 'Tis the stamp
    Of God's true life to be in dying brave.
'I fear not death, but dying' – not the long
    Hereafter, sweetened by immortal love;
But the quick, terrible last breath – the strong
    Convulsion. Oh, my Lord of breath above!
Grant me a quiet end, in easeful rest –
A sweet removal, on my mother's breast.

October's gold is dim – the forests rot,
    The weary rain falls ceaseless, while the day
    Is wrapp'd in damp. In mire of village way
The hedgerow leaves are stamped, and, all forgot,
The broodless nest sits visible in the thorn.
    Autumn, among her drooping marigolds,
    Weeps all her garnered sheaves, and empty folds,
And dripping orchards – plundered and forlorn.
The season is a dead one, and I die!
    No more, no more for me the spring shall make
    A resurrection in the earth and take
The death from out her heart – O God, I die!
The cold throat-mist creeps nearer, till I breathe
Corruption. Drop, stark night, upon my death!

JOHN BETJEMAN

Inevitable

First there was putting hot-water bottles to it,
 Then there was seeing what an osteopath could do,
Then trying drugs to coax the thing and woo it,
 Then came the time when he knew that he was through.

Now in his hospital bed I see him lying
 Limp on the pillows like a cast-off Teddy bear.
Is he too ill to know that he is dying?
 And, if he does know, does he really care?

Grey looks the ward with November's overcasting
 But his large eyes seem to see beyond the day;
Speech becomes sacred near silence everlasting
 Oh if I *must* speak, have I words to say?

In the past weeks we had talked about Variety,
 Vesta Victoria, Lew Lake and Wilkie Bard,
Horse-buses, hansoms, crimes in High Society –
 Although we knew his death was near, we fought against
 it hard.

Now from his remoteness in a stillness unaccountable
 He drags himself to earth again to say goodbye to me –
His final generosity when almost insurmountable
 The barriers and mountains he has crossed again must
 be.

JOHN MILTON

On His Blindness

When I consider how my light is spent,
   Ere half my days in this dark world and wide,
   And that one talent which is death to hide
   Lodged with me useless, though my soul more bent
To serve therewith my Maker, and present
   My true account, lest he returning chide,
   'Doth God exact day-labour, light denied?'
   I fondly ask. But Patience, to prevent
That murmur, soon replies, 'God doth not need
   Either man's work or his own gifts; who best
   Bear his mild yoke, they serve him best. His state
Is kingly: thousands at his bidding speed,
   And post o'er land and ocean without rest;
   They also serve who only stand and wait.'

W.H. AUDEN

Funeral Blues

Stop all the clocks, cut off the telephone,
Prevent the dog from barking with a juicy bone,
Silence the pianos and with muffled drum
Bring out the coffin, let the mourners come.

Let aeroplanes circle moaning overhead
Scribbling on the sky the message He Is Dead,
Put crêpe bows round the white necks of
   the public doves,
Let the traffic policemen wear black cotton gloves.

He was my North, my South, my East and West,
My working week and my Sunday rest,
My noon, my midnight, my talk, my song;
I thought that love would last for ever: I was wrong.

The stars are not wanted now: put out every one;
Pack up the moon and dismantle the sun;
Pour away the ocean and sweep up the wood;
For nothing now can ever come to any good.

ROBERT FALCON SCOTT

The Death of Captain Oates
from *Scott's Last Expedition*

Tragedy all along the line. At lunch, the day before yesterday, poor Titus Oates said he couldn't go on; he proposed we should leave him in his sleeping-bag. That we could not do, and we induced him to come on, on the afternoon march. In spite of its awful nature for him he struggled on and we made a few miles. At night he was worse and we knew the end had come.

Should this be found I want these facts recorded. Oates' last thoughts were of his Mother, but immediately before he took pride in thinking that his regiment would be pleased with the bold way in which he met his death. We can testify to his bravery. He has borne intense suffering for weeks without complaint, and to the very last was able and willing to discuss outside subjects. He did not – would not – give up hope till the very end. He was a brave soul. This was the end. He slept through the night before last, hoping not to wake; but he woke in the morning – yesterday. It was blowing a blizzard. He said, 'I am just going outside and may be some time.' He went out into the blizzard and we have not seen him since.

I take this opportunity of saying that we have stuck to our sick companions to the last. In case of Edgar Evans, when absolutely out of food and he lay insensible, the safety of the remainder seemed to demand his abandonment, but Providence mercifully removed him at this critical moment. He died a natural death, and we did not leave him till two hours after his death.

We knew that poor Oates was walking to his death, but though we tried to dissuade him, we knew it was the act of a brave man and an English gentleman. We all hope to meet the end with a similar spirit, and assuredly the end is not far.

March 29 – Since the 21st we have had a continuous gale from W.S.W. and S.W. We had fuel to make two cups of tea apiece, and bare food for two days on the 20th. Every day we have been ready to start for our depot *eleven miles away*, but outside the door of the tent it remains a scene of whirling drift. I do not think we can hope for any better things now. We shall stick it out to the end, but we are getting weaker, of course, and the end cannot be far.

It seems a pity, but I do not think I can write more.

R. Scott

Last entry:
For God's sake look after our people.

ALFRED, LORD TENNYSON

from *In Memoriam, A.H.H.*

Dark house, by which once more I stand
   Here in the long unlovely street,
   Doors, where my heart was used to beat
So quickly, waiting for a hand,

A hand that can be clasped no more –
   Behold me, for I cannot sleep,
   And like a guilty thing I creep
At earliest morning to the door.

He is not here; but far away
   The noise of life begins again,
   And ghastly through the drizzling rain
On the bald street breaks the blank day.

SIEGFRIED SASSOON

Does It Matter?

Does it matter? – losing your legs? . . .
For people will always be kind,
And you need not show that you mind
When the others come in after hunting
To gobble their muffins and eggs.

Does it matter? – losing your sight? . . .
There's such splendid work for the blind;
And people will always be kind,
As you sit on the terrace remembering
And turning your face to the light.

Do they matter? – those dreams from the pit? . . .
You can drink and forget and be glad,
And people won't say that you're mad;
For they'll know you've fought for your country
And no one will worry a bit.

GEORGE ELIOT

from *Silas Marner*

Anyone who had looked at him as the red light shone upon his pale face, strange straining eyes, and meagre form, would perhaps have understood the mixture of contemptuous pity, dread, and suspicion with which he was regarded by his neighbours in Raveloe. Yet few men could be more harmless than poor Marner. In his truthful simple soul, not even the growing greed and worship of gold could beget any vice directly injurious to others. The light of his faith quite put out, and his affections made desolate, he had clung with all the force of his nature to his work and his money; and like all objects to which a man devotes himself, they had fashioned him into correspondence with themselves. His loom, as he wrought in it without ceasing, had in its turn wrought on him, and confirmed more and more the monotonous craving for its monotonous response. His gold, as he hung over it and saw it grow, gathered his power of loving together into a hard isolation like its own.

As soon as he was warm he began to think it would be a long while to wait till after supper before he drew out his guineas, and it would be pleasant to see them on the table before him as he ate his unwonted feast. For joy is the best of wine, and Silas's guineas were a golden wine of that sort.

He rose and placed his candle unsuspectingly on the floor

near his loom, swept away the sand without noticing any change, and removed the bricks. The sight of the empty hole made his heart leap violently, but the belief that his gold was gone could not come at once – only terror, and the eager effort to put an end to the terror. He passed his trembling hand all about the hole, trying to think it possible that his eyes had deceived him; then he held the candle in the hole and examined it curiously, trembling more and more. At last he shook so violently that he let fall the candle, and lifted his hands to his head, trying to steady himself, that he might think. Had he put his gold somewhere else, by a sudden resolution last night, and then forgotten it? A man falling into dark waters seeks a momentary footing even on sliding stones; and Silas, by acting as if he believed in false hopes, warded off the moment of despair. He searched in every corner, he turned his bed over, and shook it, and kneaded it; he looked in his brick oven where he laid his sticks. When there was no other place to be searched, he kneeled down again and felt once more all round the hole. There was no untried refuge left for a moment's shelter from the terrible truth.

Yes, there was a sort of refuge which always comes with the prostration of thought under an overpowering passion: it was that expectation of impossibilities, that belief in contradictory images, which is still distinct from madness, because it is capable of being dissipated by the external fact. Silas got up from his knees trembling, and looked round at the table: didn't the gold lie there after all? The table was bare. Then he turned and looked behind him – looked all round his dwelling, seeming to strain his brown eyes after some possible appearance of the bags where he had already sought them in vain. He could see every object in his cottage – and his gold was not there.

Again he put his trembling hands to his head, and gave a wild ringing scream, the cry of desolation. For a few moments after, he stood motionless; but the cry had relieved him from the first maddening pressure of the truth.

He turned, and tottered towards his loom, and got into the seat where he worked, instinctively seeking this as the strongest assurance of reality.

. . . During the last few weeks, since he had lost his money, he had contracted the habit of opening his door and looking out from time to time, as if he thought that his money might be somehow coming back to him, or that some trace, some news of it, might be mysteriously on the road, and be caught by the listening ear or the straining eye. It was chiefly at night, when he was not occupied in his loom, that he fell into this repetition of an act for which he could have assigned no definite purpose, and which can hardly be understood except by those who have undergone a bewildering separation from a supremely loved object. In the evening twilight, and later whenever the night was not dark, Silas looked out on that narrow prospect round the Stone-pits, listening and gazing, not with hope, but with mere yearning and unrest.

This morning he had been told by some of his neighbours that it was New Year's Eve, and that he must sit up and hear the old year rung out and the new rung in, because that was good luck, and might bring his money back again. This was only a friendly Raveloe-way of jesting with the half-crazy oddities of a miser, but it had perhaps helped to throw Silas into a more than usually excited state. Since the oncoming of twilight he had opened his door again and again, though only to shut it immediately at seeing all distance veiled by the falling snow. But the last time he opened it the snow had ceased, and the clouds were parting here and there. He stood and listened, and gazed for a long while – there was really something on the road coming towards him then, but he caught no sign of it: and the stillness and the wide trackless snow seemed to narrow his solitude, and touched his yearning with the chill of despair. He went in again and put his right hand on the latch of the door to close it – but he did not close it: he was arrested, as he had been already since his loss, by the invisible wand of catalepsy, and stood like a graven image, with wide but sightless eyes, holding open his door, powerless to resist either the good or evil that might enter there.

MARTIAL

Erotion

To you, my father, Fronto, and to you, my mother, Flaccilla,
I entrust this little girl, my darling and my delight. May
Erotion not grow pale in fear of the black shadows and the
portentous jaws of the hound of Tartarus. She would have
just survived the chill of her sixth winter, had she but lived
just so many days more. Now let her frolic and play with her
guardians so old and prattle my name with lisping tongue.
Let not hard turf cover her tender bones, and be not heavy
on her, O earth; she was not heavy on you.

THOMAS NASHE

In Time of Pestilence

Adieu, farewell earth's bliss;
This world uncertain is;
Fond are life's lustful joys;
Death proves them all but toys;
None from his darts can fly;
I am sick, I must die.
    Lord, have mercy on us!

Rich men, trust not in wealth,
Gold cannot buy you health;
Physic himself must fade.
All things to end are made,
The plague full swift goes by;
I am sick, I must die.
    Lord, have mercy on us!

Beauty is but a flower
Which wrinkles will devour;
Brightness falls from the air;
Queens have died young and fair;
Dust hath closed Helen's eye.
I am sick, I must die.
    Lord, have mercy on us!

Strength stoops unto the grave,
Worms feed on Hector brave;
Swords may not fight with fate,
Earth still holds ope her gate.
'Come, come' the bells do cry.
I am sick, I must die.
    Lord, have mercy on us.

Wit with his wantonness
Tasteth death's bitterness;
Hell's executioner
Hath no ears for to hear
What vain art can reply.
I am sick, I must die.
    Lord have mercy on us.

Haste, therefore, each degree,
To welcome destiny;
Heaven is our heritage,
Earth but a player's stage;
Mount we unto the sky.
I am sick, I must die.
    Lord, have mercy on us.

SIR THOMAS MALORY

The Death of Lancelot

Than wente syr Bors unto syr Ector and tolde hym how there laye hys brother, syr Launcelot, dede. And than syr Ector threwe hys shelde, swerde, and helme from hym, and whan he behelde syr Launcelottes vysage he fyl down in a swoun. And whan he waked it were harde ony tonge to telle the doleful complayntes that he made for hys brother.

'A, Launcelot!' he sayd, 'thou were hede of al Crysten knyghtes! And now I dare say,' sayd syr Ector, 'thou syr Launcelot, there thou lyest, that thou were never matched of erthely knyghtes hande. And thou were the curtest knyght that ever bare shelde! And thou were the truest frende to thy lovar that ever bestrade hors, and thou were the trewest lover of a synful man that ever loved woman, and thou were the kyndest man that ever strake wyth swerde. And thou were the godelyest persone that ever cam emonge prees of knyghtes, and thou was the mekest man and the jentyllest that ever ete in halle emonge ladyes, and thou were the sternest knyght to thy mortal foo that ever put spere in the reeste.'

Than there was wepyng and dolour out of mesure.

A.E. HOUSMAN

The Sigh that Heaves the Grasses

The sigh that heaves the grasses,
  Whence thou wilt never rise
Is of the air that passes
  And knows not if it sighs.

The diamond tears adorning
  Thy low mound on the lea,
Those are the tears of morning,
  That weeps, but not for thee.

ANTON CHEKHOV

from *Three Sisters*

The three sisters stand with their arms round one another:

MASHA: Oh, listen to that band! They are going away from us; one has gone altogether, gone forever. We are left alone to begin our life over again ... We've got to live ... we've got to live ...

IRINA: (*lays her head on* OLGA'S *bosom*): A time will come when everyone will know what all this is for, why there is this misery; there will be no mysteries and, meanwhile, we have got to live ... we have got to work, only to work! Tomorrow I shall go alone; I shall teach in the school, and I will give all my life to those to whom it may be of use. Now it's autumn; soon winter will come and cover us with snow, and I will work, I will work.

OLGA (*embraces both her sisters*): The music is so gay, so confident, and one longs for life! O my God! Time will pass, and we shall go away for ever, and we shall be forgotten, our faces will be forgotten, our voices, and how many there were of us; but our sufferings will pass into joy for those who will live after us, happiness and peace will be established upon earth, and they will remember kindly and bless those who have lived before. O dear sisters, our life is not ended yet. We shall live! The music is so gay, so joyful, and it seems as though a little more and we shall know what we are

48

living for, why we are suffering . . . If we only knew – if we only knew!

The music grows more and more subdued; KULIGIN, *cheerful and smiling, brings the hat and cape;* ANDREY *pushes the perambulator in which Bobik is sitting.*

TCHEBUTYKIN (*humming softly*): 'Tarara-boom-dee-ay!' (*reads his paper*). It doesn't matter, it doesn't matter.

OLGA: If we only knew, if we only knew!

WALT WHITMAN

from *Song of Myself*

A child said, *What is the grass?* fetching it to me with full
   hands;
How could I answer the child? I do not know what it is any
   more than he.

I guess it must be the flag of my disposition, out of hopeful
   green stuff woven.

Or I guess it is the handkerchief of the Lord,
A scented gift and remembrancer designedly dropt,
Bearing the owner's name someway in the corners, that we
   may see and remark, and say *Whose?*

Or, I guess the grass is itself a child, the produced babe of the
   vegetation.

Or I guess it is a uniform hieroglyphic,
And it means, Sprouting alike in broad zones and narrow
   zones,
Growing among black folks as among white,
Kanuck, Tuckahoe, Congressman, Cuff, I give them the
   same, I receive them the same.

And now it seems to me the beautiful uncut hair of graves.
Tenderly will I use you curling grass,

It may be you transpire from the breasts of young men,
It may be if I had known them I would have loved them,
It may be you are from old people, or from offspring taken
    soon out of their mothers' laps,
And here you are the mothers' laps.

This grass is very dark to be from the white heads of old
    mothers,
Darker than the colourless beards of old men,
Dark to come from under the faint red roofs of mouths.
O I perceive after all so many uttering tongues,
And I perceive they do not come from the roofs of mouths
    for nothing.

I wish I could translate the hints about the dead young men
    and women,
And the hints about old men and mothers, and the offspring
    taken soon out of their laps.

What do you think has become of the young and old men?
And what do you think has become of the women and
    children?

They are alive and well somewhere,
The smallest sprout shows there is really no death,
And if ever there was it led forward life, and does not wait at
    the end to arrest it,
And ceas'd the moment life appear'd.

All goes onward and outward, nothing collapses,
And to die is different from what any one supposed, and
    luckier.

EZRA POUND

Ione, Dead the Long Year

Empty are the ways,
Empty are the ways of this land
And the flowers
      Bend over with heavy heads.
They bend in vain.
Empty are the ways of this land
      Where Ione
Walked once, and now does not walk
But seems like a person just gone.

NELL STROUD

Her Mother (from *The Josser*)

Sometimes, sitting in the box office, I think about mum, and what happened to her, how she suddenly went away and returned a different person, I remember her voice and her laugh and the way she hugged me, and I cannot believe it. The things she would say, the intrigue of her thoughts and the world around her, that is all gone too. What we were to her and her vision of life. Just the person who is always there. She would say to us, don't just think of your great aunts as being old people, they were young and adventurous like you once, young girls, and I see now what she meant. I wish that she was still here. I cry for her counsel. I think of the fact that she has gone and sometimes I actually say no out loud, as if that will make any difference. Why won't she walk into the room now? Her quick strong walk and big smile, pleased to see you, never let the sun go down on your anger, girls.

She is about thirty and she is standing beside a car, a Citroën. All the doors are wide open and the bonnet is open too. She has got her back to the car and her hand on her hip and her feet are neatly together, stripy tights and a denim skirt and sensible shoes, a jersey with the sleeves rolled up and a belt around the jersey. Her other hand is resting on the edge of the pram and she is looking down at her dog who is looning about, looking down and saying something and smiling. She is surrounded by baskets and bags all sitting in the gravel, loose clothes, and the pram is full of stuff too, saddles, riding hats, blankets, and more bits of wicker basket, fragments and suggestions of more luggage. I can't think how she is going to get it all into the car, the pram and the dog and everything, and the car looks totally weighed down already. It is so typical though, she looks totally relaxed, talking to the dog, her feet together so neatly. A world goes past and we never even realise it.

DANTE ALIGHIERI

from *The Inferno* (Canto 5)

And now I can hear the notes of agony

In sad crescendo beginning to reach my ear;
    Now I am where the noise of lamentation
    Comes at me in blasts of sorrow. I am where

All light is mute, with a bellowing like the ocean
    Turbulent in a storm of warring winds,
    The hurricane of Hell in perpetual motion

Sweeping the ravaged spirits as it rends,
    Twists, and torments them. Driven as if to land,
    They reach the ruin: groaning, tears, laments,

And cursing of the power of Heaven. I learned
    They suffer here who sinned in carnal things –
    Their reason mastered by desire, suborned.

As winter starlings riding on their wings
    Form crowded flocks, so spirits dip and veer
    Foundering in the wind's rough buffetings,

Upward or downward, driven here and there
    With never ease from pain nor hope of rest.
    As chanting cranes will form a line in air,

55

So I saw souls come uttering cries – wind-tossed,
   And lofted by the storm. 'Master,' I cried,
     'Who are these people, by black air oppressed?'

'First among these you wish to know,' he said,
   'Was empress of many tongues – she so embraced
     Lechery that she decreed it justified

Legally, to evade the scandal of her lust:
   She is that Semiramis of whom we read,
     Successor and wife of Ninus, she possessed

The lands the Sultan rules. Next, she who died
   By her own hand for love, and broke her vow
     To Sychaeus's ashes. After her comes lewd

And wanton Cleopatra. See Helen, too,
   Who caused a cycle of many evil years;
     And great Achilles, the hero whom love slew

In his last battle. Paris and Tristan are here – '
   He pointed out by name a thousand souls
     Whom love had parted from our life, or more.

THOMAS MOORE

The Last Rose of Summer

'Tis the last rose of summer
   Left blooming alone;
All her lovely companions
   Are faded and gone;
No flower of her kindred,
   No rose-bud is nigh,
To reflect back her blushes,
   Or give sigh for sigh.

I'll not leave thee, thou lone one!
   To pine on the stem;
Since the lovely are sleeping,
   Go, sleep thou with them.
Thus kindly I scatter
   Thy leaves o'er the bed
Where thy maids of the garden
   Lie scentless and dead.

So soon may I follow,
   When friendships decay,
And from Love's shining circle
   The gems drop away.
When true hearts lie withered,
   And fond ones are flown,
O! who would inhabit
   This bleak world alone?

HELEN THOMAS

from *World Without End*

'And here are my poems, I've copied them all out in this book for you, and the last of all is for you. I wrote it last night, but don't read it now . . . It's still freezing. The ground is like iron, and more snow has fallen. The children will come to the station with me; and now I must be off.'

We were alone in my room. He took me in his arms, holding me tightly to him, his face white, his eyes full of a fear I had never seen before. My arms were round his neck. 'Beloved, I love you,' was all I could say. 'Helen, Helen, Helen,' he said, 'remember that, whatever happens, all is well between us for ever and ever.' And hand in hand we went downstairs and out to the children, who were playing in the snow.

A thick mist hung everywhere, and there was no sound except, far away in the valley, a train shunting. I stood at the gate watching him go; he turned back to wave until the mist and the hill hid him. I heard his old call coming up to me: 'Coo-ee!' he called. 'Coo-ee!' I answered, keeping my voice strong to call again. Again through the muffled air came his 'Coo-ee'. And again went my answer like an echo. 'Coo-ee' came fainter next time with the hill between us, but my 'Coo-ee' went out of my lungs strong to pierce to him as he strode away from me. 'Coo-ee!' So faint now, it might be only my own call flung back from the thick air and muffling snow. I put my hands up to my mouth to make a trumpet, but no sound came. Panic seized me, and I ran through the mist and the snow to the top of the hill, and stood there a moment dumbly, with straining eyes and ears. There was nothing but the mist and the snow and the silence of death.

Then with leaden feet which stumbled in a sudden darkness that overwhelmed me I groped my way back to the empty house.

DYLAN THOMAS

'Do not go gentle into that good night'

Do not go gentle into that good night,
Old age should burn and rave at close of day;
Rage, rage against the dying of the light.

Though wise men at their end know dark is right,
Because their words had forked no lightning they
Do not go gentle into that good night.

Good men, the last wave by, crying how bright
Their frail deeds might have danced in a green bay,
Rage, rage against the dying of the light.

Wild men who caught and sang the sun in flight,
And learn, too late, they grieved it on its way,
Do not go gentle into that good night.

Grave men, near death, who see with blinding sight
Blind eyes could blaze like meteors and be gay,
Rage, rage against the dying of the light.

And you, my father, there on the sad height,
Curse, bless, me now with your fierce tears, I pray.
Do not go gentle into that good night.
Rage, rage against the dying of the light.

JOHN DONNE

The Computation

For the first twenty years, since yesterday,
I scarce believed thou couldst be gone away;
For forty more, I fed on favours past,
And forty on hopes – that thou wouldst, they might, last.
Tears drowned one hundred, and sighs blew out two;
A thousand, I did neither think, nor do,
Or not divide, all being one thought of you;
Or in a thousand more forgot that too.
Yet call not this long life, but think that I
Am, by being dead, immortal. Can ghosts die?

SENECA

On Death

No one is so ignorant as not to know that he must die one day; yet when a man comes near to it, he turns his back, trembles, and laments. Would you not consider that man to be the most foolish of all men, who weeps because he was not alive a thousand years ago? A man is just as foolish if he weeps because he will not be alive a thousand years from now. These examples are parallel; you will not be and you were not. Neither of these two times has anything to do with you. You have been thrown into this moment, and if you would extend it, how far will you do so? Why are you weeping? What do you want? You are wasting your pains.

Cease to hope that by prayer you can alter the rulings of heaven.

The rulings are settled and fixed and drawn by a mighty and everlasting inevitability. You will go where all things go. What is there new in this for you? You were born subject to this law. This happened to your father, your mother, your ancestors, everyone who came before you; it will happen to everyone who comes after you. A succession that is never broken and which no power can change has bound all things and draws them along. What a vast number of people who must die will follow you! What a large number will accompany you! You would be braver, maybe, if you had many thousands dying with you: and yet at this very instant when you are shrinking from dying, many thousands both of men and of animals are breathing out their life in different ways. But did you imagine that you yourself would not at some time reach that point to which you were always travelling? There is no journey without an ending.

ROBERT HERRICK

To a Gentlewoman Objecting to Him
His Grey Hairs

Am I despised because you say,
And I dare swear, that I am grey?
Know, lady, you have but your day,
And time will come when you shall wear
Such frost and snow upon your hair.
And when (though long) it comes to pass
You question with your looking-glass,
And in that sincere crystal seek
But find no rosebud in your cheek,
Nor any bed to give the show
Where such a rare Carnation grew,
And such a smiling Tulip too,
Ah! then too late, close in your chamber keeping,
    It will be told
    That you are old,
By those true tears y'are weeping.

DAVID WRIGHT

Et in Arcadia

Living is here
And now. I
Look forward, see
Today tomorrow
A yesterday
Of what was I
When we were.

All is recalling: how
Our vision of what's gone
Changes with each new Now
As we change with what's done
And our perspectives change.
Life, they say, must go on
To alter all, to alter
In recollection
That shadow of her shadow,
All of her that I am.

The sun on a polluted river,
May morning by a flowing Thames,
A lace of trees, their leaves beginning,
And we two strangers holding hands
Beside a theatre yet a-building,
By broken bricks and iron bones

Of weathered bomb-sites weeding over
In sunlight that's presaging summer,
A summer that has come, and gone.

Et in Arcadia
Ego. As evening
Leads her shadow on
And, diamond, a star
Increases with the wane
Of light to promise a
Different beginning,
I am to thank whatever for
The fortune of day.

I am changing: she does not.
How can I change and she not change?
Those words, Till death do us part,
Too late I understand.
I see things in a different dark,
All things that nothing can explain.

BEN JONSON   ·

My Picture Left in Scotland

I now thinke, Love is rather deafe, than blind,
　　For else it could not be,
　　　　That she,
Whom I adore so much, should so slight me,
　　And cast my love behind:
I'm sure my language to her, was as sweet,
　　And every close did meet
　　In sentence, of as subtile feet,
　　　　As hath the youngest Hee,
　　That sits in shadow of Apollo's tree.
Oh, but my conscious feares,
　　　　That flie my thoughts betweene,
　　　　Tell me that she hath seene
　　My hundreds of grey haires,
　　Told seven and fortie yeares.
Read so much wast, as she cannot imbrace
My mountaine belly, and my rockie face,
And all these through her eyes, have stopt her eares.

C.P. CAVAFY

The City

You said: 'I'll go to another land, go to another sea,
find some other town better than this one.
Fated, condemned, is all that I've ever done
and my heart, like a dead body, is buried in a tomb.
How long must my mind remain within this gloom?
When I cast my eyes about me, look no matter where,
I see the black ruins of my life, here,
where I've spent so many years – wasted them, destroyed
   them utterly.'

You will not find new lands, not find another sea.
The city will follow you. You'll wander down
these very streets, age in these same quarters of the town,
among the same houses finally turn grey.
You'll reach this city always. Don't hope to get away:
for you there is no ship, no road anywhere.
As you've destroyed your life here,
in this small corner, so in the whole world you've wrecked it
   utterly.

ALBERT CAMUS

His Father's Grave (from *The First Man*)

The caretaker opened a large book bound in wrapping paper and with his dirty finger went down a list of names. His finger came to a stop. 'Cormery Henri,' he said, 'fatally wounded at the Battle of the Marne, died at Saint-Brieuc 11 October 1914.'

'That's it,' said the traveller.

The caretaker closed the book. 'Come,' he said. And he led the way to the first row of gravestones, some of them simple, others ugly and pretentious, all covered with that bead and marble bric-à-brac that would disgrace any place on earth. 'Was he related to you?' he asked absently.

'He was my father.'

'That's rough,' the other man said.

'No, it isn't. I was less than a year old when he died. So, you see.'

'Yes,' said the caretaker, 'but even so. Too many died.'

Jacques Cormery did not answer. Surely, too many had died, but, as to his father, he could not muster a filial devotion he did not feel. For all these years he had been living in France, he had promised himself to do what his mother, who stayed in Algeria, what she [*sic*] for such a long time had been asking him to do: visit the grave of his father that she herself had never seen. He thought this visit made no sense, first of all for himself, who had never known his father, who knew next to nothing of what he had been, and who loathed conventional gestures and behaviour; and then for his mother, who never spoke of the dead man and could picture nothing of what he was going to see. But since his old mentor had retired to Saint-Brieuc and so he would have an opportunity to see him again, Cormery had made up his mind to go and visit this dead stranger, and had even insisted on doing it before joining his old friend so that afterwards he would feel completely free.

'It's here,' said the caretaker. They had arrived at a square-shaped area, enclosed by small markers of grey stone connected with a heavy chain that had been painted black. The gravestones – and they were many – were all alike: plain inscribed rectangles set at equal intervals row on row. Each grave was decorated with a small bouquet of fresh flowers. 'For forty years the French Remembrance has been responsible for the upkeep. Look, here he is.' He indicated a stone in the first row. Jacques Cormery stopped at some distance from the grave. 'I'll leave you,' the caretaker said.

Cormery approached the stone and gazed vacantly at it. Yes, that was indeed his name. He looked up. Small white and grey clouds were passing slowly across the sky, which was paler now, and from it fell a light that was alternately bright and overcast. Around him, in the vast field of the dead, silence reigned. Nothing but a muffled murmur from the town came over the high walls. Occasionally a black silhouette would pass among the distant graves. Jacques Cormery, gazing up at the slow navigation of the clouds across the sky, was trying to discern, beyond the odour of damp flowers, the salty smell just then coming from the distant motionless sea when the clink of a bucket against the marble of a tombstone drew him from his reverie. At that moment he read on the tomb the date of his father's birth, which he now discovered he had not known. Then he read the two dates, '1885–1914', and automatically did the arithmetic: twenty-nine years. Suddenly he was struck by an idea that shook his very body. He was forty years old.

The man buried under that slab, who had been his father, was younger than he.

And the wave of tenderness and pity that at once filled his heart was not the stirring of the soul that leads the son to the memory of the vanished father, but the overwhelming compassion that a grown man feels for an unjustly murdered child – something here was not in the natural order and, in truth, there was no order but only madness and chaos when the son was older than the father. The course of time itself was shattering around him while he remained motionless among those tombs he now no longer saw, and the years no longer kept to their places in the great river that flows to its end. They were no more than waves and surf and eddies where Jacques Cormery was now struggling in the grip of anguish and pity. He looked at the other inscriptions in that section and realised from the dates that this soil was strewn with children who had been the fathers of greying men who thought they were living in this present time. For he too believed he was living, he alone had created himself, he knew his own strength, his vigour, he could cope and he had himself well in hand. But, in the strange dizziness of that moment, the statue every man eventually erects and that hardens in the fire of the years, into which he then creeps and there awaits its final crumbling – that statue was rapidly cracking, it was already collapsing. All that was left was this anguished heart, eager to live, rebelling against the deadly order of the world that had been with him for forty years, and still struggling against the wall that separated him from the secret of all life, wanting to go farther, to go beyond, and to discover, discover before dying, discover at last in order to be, just once to be, for a single second, but for ever.

He looked back on his life, a life that had been foolish, courageous, cowardly, wilful, and always straining towards that goal which he knew nothing about, and actually that life had all gone by without his having tried to imagine who this man was who had given him that life and then

71

immediately had gone off to die in a strange land on the other side of the seas. At twenty-nine, had he himself not been frail, been ailing, tense, stubborn, sensual, dreamy, cynical, and brave? Yes, he had been all that and much else besides; he had been alive, in short had been a man, and yet he had never thought of the man who slept there as a living being, but as a stranger who passed by on the land where he himself was born, of whom his mother said that he looked like him and that he died on the field of battle. Yet the secret he had eagerly sought to learn through books and people now seemed to him to be intimately linked with this dead man, this younger father, with what he had been and what he had become, and it seemed that he himself had gone far afield in search of what was close to him in time and in blood. To tell the truth, he had received no help. In a family where they spoke little, where no one read or wrote, with an unhappy and listless mother, who would have informed him about this young and pitiable father? No one had known him but his mother and she had forgotten him. Of that he was sure. And he had died unknown on this earth where he had fleetingly passed, like a stranger. No doubt it was up to him to ask, to inform himself. But for someone like him, who has nothing and wants the world entire, all his energy is not enough to create himself and to conquer or to understand that world. After all, it was not too late; he could still search, he could learn who this man had been who now seemed closer to him than any other being on this earth. He could . . .

Now the afternoon was coming to its end. The rustle of a skirt, a black shadow, brought him back to the landscape of tombs and sky that surrounded him. He had to leave; there was nothing more for him to do here. But he could not turn away from this name, those dates. Under that slab were left only ashes and dust. But, for him, his father was again alive, a strange silent life, and it seemed to him that again he was going to forsake him, to leave his father to haunt yet another night the endless solitude he had been hurled into and then deserted. The empty sky resounded with a sudden loud explosion: an invisible aeroplane had crossed the sound barrier. Turning his back on the grave, Jacques Cormery abandoned his father.

WILLIAM SHAKESPEARE

Sonnet 73

That time of year thou mayst in me behold
When yellow leaves, or none, or few, do hang
Upon those boughs which shake against the cold,
Bare ruin'd choirs, where late the sweet birds sang.
In me thou see'st the twilight of such day
As after sunset fadeth in the west;
Which by and by black night doth take away,
Death's second self, that seals up all in rest.
In me thou see'st the glowing of such fire,
That on the ashes of his youth doth lie,
As the death-bed whereon it must expire,
Consumed with that which it was nourish'd by.
   This thou perceiv'st, which makes thy love more strong,
   To love that well which thou must leave ere long.

OLIVER BERNARD

That Penknife

That penknife lies in the long grass where I lost it,
But it is closer in my hand for that.
This child's tears have rusted it to a powder
The dew keeps dark and rain has battered flat;
Earth of red oxide; and somewhere a curled, peeling
Sliver of bone: the handle. What did I lose?
– What went into it. That comes back now, heavily
Held, and solid as then. But it hurt like a bruise
At the time, and worse than a bruise it wasn't there
To be touched and pondered over; till today.
There it lay in the grass. I wonder whether
It's true what all of us hoped when we used to say
To a marble: *Brother go and find your brother*.
Does it work? But marbles are common: you can't play
Like that with a penknife when you have no other.

GEORGE PEELE

Farewell to Arms
to Queen Elizabeth

His golden locks time hath to silver turned;
    O time too swift, O swiftness never ceasing!
His youth 'gainst time and age hath ever spurned,
    But spurned in vain; youth waneth by increasing:
Beauty, strength, youth, are flowers but fading seen;
Duty, faith, love, are roots, and ever green.

His helmet now shall make a hive for bees;
    And, lovers' sonnets turned to holy psalms,
A man-at-arms must now serve on his knees,
    And feed on prayers, which are age's alms:
But though from court to cottage he depart,
His saint is sure of his unspotted heart.

And when he saddest sits in homely cell,
    He'll teach his swains this carol for a song:
'Blest be the hearts that wish my sovereign well,
    Curst be the souls that think her any wrong.'
Goddess, allow this aged man his right,
To be your beadsman now, that was your knight.

JOHN PUDNEY

For Johnny

Do not despair
For Johnny-head-in-air;
He sleeps as sound
As Johnny underground.

Fetch out no shroud
For Johnny-in-the-cloud;
And keep your tears
For him in after years.

Better by far
For Johnny-the-bright-star,
To keep your head,
And see his children fed.

JOHN DRYDEN

Chorus from *The Secular Masque*

All, all of a piece throughout:
Thy chase had a beast in view;
Thy wars brought nothing about;
Thy lovers were all untrue.
'Tis well an old age is out,
And time to begin a new.

SIR THOMAS WYATT

'They Flee From Me'

They flee from me that sometime did me seek
With naked foot stalking in my chamber.
I have seen them gentle, tame and meek
That now are wild and do not remember
That sometime they put themselves in danger
To take bread at my hand; and now they range
Busily seeking with a continual change.

Thanked be fortune, it hath been otherwise
Twenty times better, but once in special,
In thin array after a pleasant guise,
When her loose gown from her shoulders did fall
And she caught me in her arms long and small,
Therewithal sweetly did me kiss
And softly said, 'Dear heart, how like you this?'

It was no dream: I lay broad waking.
But all is turned thorough my gentleness
Into a strange fashion of forsaking.
And I have leave to go of her goodness
And she also to use newfangleness.
But since that I so kindly am served
I would fain know what she hath deserved.

WILFRED OWEN

Anthem for Doomed Youth

What passing-bells for these who die as cattle?
  Only the monstrous anger of the guns.
  Only the stuttering rifles' rapid rattle
Can patter out their hasty orisons.
No mockeries now for them; no prayers nor bells;
  Nor any voice of mourning save the choirs, –
The shrill, demented choirs of wailing shells;
  And bugles calling for them from sad shires.

What candles may be held to speed them all?
  Not in the hands of boys, but in their eyes
Shall shine the holy glimmers of goodbyes.
  The pallor of girls' brows shall be their pall;
Their flowers the tenderness of patient minds,
And each slow dusk a drawing-down of blinds.

WILLIAM BELL

On a Dying Boy

Oh leave his body broken on the rocks
where fainting sense may drown beneath the sound
of the complaining surf. His spirit mocks
our ignorant attempts to hem it round:
as eagerly as body sought the ground
into its native ocean must it flow.
Oh let his body lie where it was found,
there's nothing we can do to help him now.

And hide his face under his tattered coat
until the women come to where he lies,
they come to bind the silence in his throat
and shut the eternal darkness in his eyes,
to wash the cold sweat of his agonies
and wash the blood that's clotted on his brow.
Cover his face from the unfriendly skies,
there's nothing we can do to help him now.

And watch even his enemies forget him,
the skies forget his sobs, the rocks his blood:
and think how neither rock nor sky dared let him
grow old enough for evil or for good;
and then forget him too. Even if we could
bring back the flower that's fallen from the bough,
bring back the flower that never left the bud,
there's nothing we can do to help him now.

The Unquiet Grave

The wind doth blow today, my love,
   And a few small drops of rain;
I never had but one true-love;
   In cold grave she was lain.

'I'll do as much for my true-love
   As any young man may;
I'll sit and mourn all at her grave
   For a twelvemonth and a day.'

The twelvemonth and a day being up,
   The dead began to speak:
'O who sits weeping on my grave,
   And will not let me sleep?' –

''Tis I, my love, sits on your grave,
   And will not let you sleep;
For I crave one kiss of your clay-cold lips,
   And that is all I seek.' –

'You crave one kiss of my clay-cold lips;
   But my breath smells earthy strong;
If you have one kiss of my clay-cold lips,
   Your time will not be long.

''Tis down in yonder garden green,
　Love, where we used to walk,
The finest flower that ere was seen
　Is wither'd to a stalk.

'The stalk is wither'd dry, my love,
　So will our hearts decay;
So make yourself content, my love,
　Till God calls you away.'

RUDYARD KIPLING

Wolf Song (from *The Jungle Book*)

What of the hunting, hunter bold?
    Brother, the watch was long and cold.
What of the quarry ye went to kill?
    Brother, he crops in the jungle still.
Where is the power that made your pride?
    Brother, it ebbs from my flank and side,
Where is the haste that ye hurry by?
    Brother, I go to my lair – to die.

MOSCHUS

Fragment of the Elegy on the Death of Bion

Ye Dorian woods and waves, lament aloud, –
Augment your tide, O streams, with fruitless tears,
For the belovèd Bion is no more.
Let every tender herb and plant and flower,
From each dejected bud and dropping bloom,
Shed dews of liquid sorrow, and with breath
Of melancholy sweetness on the wind
Diffuse its languid love; let roses blush,
Anemones grow paler for the loss
Their dells have known; and thou, O hyacinth,
Utter thy legend now – yet more, dumb flower,
Than 'Ah! alas!' – thine is no common grief –
Bion the sweetest singer is no more.

A.E. HOUSMAN

Tell Me Not Here

Tell me not here, it needs not saying,
   What tune the enchantress plays
In aftermaths of soft September
   Or under blanching mays,
For she and I were long acquainted
   And I knew all her ways.

On russet floors, by waters idle,
   The pine lets fall its cone;
The cuckoo shouts all day at nothing
   In leafy dells alone;
And traveller's joy beguiles in autumn
   Hearts that have lost their own.

On acres of the seeded grasses
   The changing burnish heaves;
Or marshalled under moons of harvest
   Stand still all night the sheaves;
Or beeches strip in storms for winter
   And stain the wind with leaves.

Possess, as I possessed a season,
   The countries I resign,
Where over elmy plains the highway
   Would mount the hills and shine,

And full of shade the pillared forest
   Would murmur and be mine.

For nature, heartless, witless nature,
   Will neither care nor know
What stranger's feet may find the meadow
   And trespass there and go,
Nor ask amid the dews of morning
   If they are mine or no.

HORACE

Lydia

The young bloods come round less often now,
Pelting your shutters and making a row
And robbing your beauty sleep. Now the door
Clings lovingly close to the jamb – though, before,

It used to move on its hinge pretty fast.
Those were the days – and they're almost past –
When lovers stood out all night long crying,
'Lydia, wake up! Save me! I'm dying!'

Soon your time's coming to be turned down
And to feel the scorn of the men about town –
A cheap hag haunting alley places
On moonless nights when the wind from Thrace is

Rising and raging, and so is the fire
In your raddled loins, the brute desire
That drives the mothers of horses mad.
You'll be lonely then and complain how sad

That the gay young boys enjoy the sheen
Of ivy best or the darker green
Of myrtle: dry old leaves they send
As a gift to the east wind, winter's friend.

JOHN HEATH-STUBBS

Address Not Known

So you are gone, and are proved bad change, as we had
    always known,
And I am left lonely in London the metropolitan city,
Perhaps to twist this incident into a durable poem –
The lesson of those who give their love to phenomenal
    beauty.

I am coming to think now that all I have loved were
    shadows
Strayed up from a dead world, through a gap in a raped
    tomb,
Or where the narcissus battens in mythological meadows:
Your face was painted upon the coffin-lid from Fayoum.

Is this my pain that is speaking? The pain was not long
    protracted:
I make a statement, forgive the betrayal, the meanness, the
    theft.
Human, I cannot suppose you had planned all that was
    enacted:
Fortitude must be procured to encounter the hollowness
    left.

The sun will not haver in its course for the lack of you,
Nor the flowers fail in colour, nor the bird stint in its song.
Only the heart that wanted somehow to have opened up
Finds the frost in the day's air, and the nights which appear
    too long.

from *The Bell Jar*

I tugged my black veil down to my chin and strode in through the wrought-iron gates. I thought it odd that in all the time my father had been buried in this graveyard, none of us had ever visited him. My mother hadn't let us come to his funeral because we were only children then, and he had died in the hospital, so the graveyard and even his death had always seemed unreal to me.

I had a great yearning, lately, to pay my father back for all the years of neglect, and start tending his grave. I had always been my father's favorite, and it seemed fitting I should take on a mourning my mother had never bothered with.

I thought that if my father hadn't died, he would have taught me all about insects, which was his specialty at the university. He would also have taught me German and Greek and Latin, which he knew, and perhaps I would be a Lutheran. My father had been a Lutheran in Wisconsin, but they were out of style in New England, so he had become a lapsed Lutheran and then, my mother said, a bitter atheist.

The graveyard disappointed me. It lay at the outskirts of the town, on low ground, like a rubbish dump, and as I walked up and down the gravel paths, I could smell the stagnant salt marshes in the distance.

The old part of the graveyard was all right, with its worn, flat stones and lichen-bitten monuments, but I soon saw my father must be buried in the modern part with dates in the nineteen forties.

The stones in the modern part were crude and cheap, and here and there a grave was rimmed with marble, like an oblong bathtub full of dirt, and rusty metal containers stuck up about where the person's navel would be, full of plastic flowers.

A fine drizzle started drifting down from the gray sky, and I grew very depressed.

I couldn't find my father anywhere.

Low, shaggy clouds scudded over that part of the horizon where the sea lay, behind the marshes and the beach shanty settlements, and raindrops darkened the black mackintosh I had bought that morning. A clammy dampness sank through to my skin.

I had asked the salesgirl, 'Is it water-repellent?'

And she had said, 'No raincoat is ever water-*repellent*. It's showerproofed.'

And when I asked her what showerproofed was, she told me I had better buy an umbrella.

But I hadn't enough money for an umbrella. What with the bus fare in and out of Boston and peanuts and newspapers and abnormal-psychology books and trips to my old home town by the sea, my New York fund was almost exhausted.

I had decided that when there was no more money in my bank account I would do it, and that morning I'd spent the last of it on the black raincoat.

Then I saw my father's gravestone.

It was crowded right up by another gravestone, head to head, the way people are crowded in a charity ward when there isn't enough space. The stone was of a mottled pink marble, like canned salmon, and all there was on it was my father's name and, under it, two dates, separated by a little dash.

At the foot of the stone I arranged the rainy armful of azaleas I had picked from a bush at the gateway of the

92

graveyard. Then my legs folded under me, and I sat down on the sopping grass. I couldn't understand why I was crying so hard.

Then I remembered that I had never cried for my father's death.

My mother hadn't cried either. She had just smiled and said what a merciful thing it was for him he had died, because if he had lived he would have been crippled and an invalid for life, and he couldn't have stood that, he would rather have died than had that happen.

I laid my face to the smooth face of the marble and howled my loss into the cold salt rain.

WILLIAM EMPSON

Let It Go

It is this deep blankness is the real thing strange.
  The more things happen to you the more you can't
    Tell or remember even what they were.

The contradictions cover such a range.
  The talk would talk and go so far aslant.
    You don't want madhouse and the whole thing there.

EMILY DICKINSON

After Great Pain

After great pain a formal feeling comes –
The nerves sit ceremonious like tombs;
The stiff Heart questions – was it He that bore?
And yesterday – or centuries before?

The feet mechanical
Go round a wooden way
Of ground or air or Ought, regardless grown,
A quartz contentment like a stone.

This is the hour of lead
Remembered if outlived,
As freezing persons recollect the snow –
First chill, then stupor, then the letting go.

LAURENCE HOPE

Kashmiri Song

Pale hands I loved beside the Shalimar,
  Where are you now? Who lies beneath your spell?
Whom do you lead on Rapture's Roadway, far,
  Before you agonise them in farewell?

Or, pale dispensers of my Joys and Pains,
  Holding the doors of Heaven and of Hell,
How the hot blood rushed wildly through the veins
  Beneath your touch, until you waved farewell.

Pale hands, pink-tipped, like Lotus buds that float
  On those cool waters where we used to dwell,
I would have rather felt you round my throat
  Crushing out life than waving me farewell!

DAVID WRIGHT

Becoming Deaf (from *Deafness*)

It was my father, looking in on his way to the office.

His visit inaugurated a ceremony which was to be observed every morning so long as I stayed at the nursing-home. Pulling his gold watch (it had rococo Victorian initials engraven on the back) from his waistcoat-pocket, he would hold it up to my ear.

'Can you hear the tick?' I would shake my head. My head was thick with bandages.

My father never failed to pay his early morning visit or to administer the ritual of the watch. It gave me a first clue to the discovery I was to make in the course of the next few weeks: that I had completely lost my hearing.

One would think that deafness must have been self-evident from the first. On the contrary it took me some time to find out what had happened. I had to deduce the fact of deafness through a process of reasoning. I did not notice it. No one inhabits a world of total silence: I had 'heard' the doctor's car driving me to the hospital, while the tread of the nurse coming into my room used to wake me in the morning – how was I to know? Nobody told me.

It was made more difficult to perceive because from the very first my eyes had unconsciously begun to translate motion into sound. My mother spent most of the day beside me and I understood everything she said. Why not? Without knowing it I had been reading her mouth all my life. When she spoke I seemed to hear her voice. It was an illusion which persisted even after I knew it was an illusion. My father, my cousin, everyone I had known, retained phantasmal voices. That they were imaginary, the projections of habit and memory, did not come home to me until I had left hospital. One day I was talking with my cousin and he, in a moment of inspiration, covered his mouth with his hand as he spoke. Silence! Once and for all I understood that when I could not see I could not hear.

But that was later. Only little by little did I attain right knowledge of my condition. The watch business put me on the track. From discovering that there were some things I could not hear I progressed to the truth that I could hear nothing.

The discovery in no way upset me. It was very gradually that I understood what had happened. Then, being innocent of experience, I was spared – as my parents certainly were not spared – speculation or foresight of the ways in which the rest of my life might be modified and hampered. For my parents what had happened was a catastrophe; to me it was an incident. It seemed neither important nor extraordinary except in so far that everything seems important and extraordinary when one is seven. Like animals, children are able to accept injuries in a casual manner, with apparent courage.

Children have a resilience and adaptability that must seem unbelievable to an adult. No courage bore me up at the age of seven; nature, or whatever you call the almost unthwartable energy of life which inhabits all young creatures – the drive to go on living under any circumstances – made deafness seem to me, at the time, one of the normal accidents of living.

In the case of a deaf child it is the parents who do the suffering, at least to begin with. Mine found themselves faced with all sorts of questions to which they had to find answers that might not, for all they knew, exist. How was I to be educated? How far would I be able to lead a 'normal' life? When I grew up, would I be capable of ordinary social intercourse? How would I earn a living? You can imagine what forebodings weighed on them. They could not know that things might work out better than they feared.

It was easier for me than for those about me to accept the fact of my deafness. How should they know I was scarcely bothered by it? In the nursing-home and during my convalescence they were continually assuring me that my hearing would come back. That I might not have been very interested one way or another, none of them guessed. I had no sense of loss. I didn't mind not hearing. Not at all! But I did begin to find it exasperating to be offered, like a never-arriving birthday treat, the prospect of some magical restoration of hearing – next week, next month, next year. Promises made in all good faith: the doctors would have proffered vague hopes. Such hopes would be handed on, transmuted to near-certainties, perhaps with the idea of keeping up my spirits. No one supposed that my spirits might have no need of being kept up – I was not in pain. I was having a jolly good time at the nursing-home. But because they were repeated so often, I at first believed the rumours and prophecies of a return of hearing. After some months, when nothing had happened, I decided that the state of suspended expectation entailed by belief in these foretellings was a nuisance. Privately and deliberately I made up my mind that no matter what anybody told me I should always be deaf.

HENRY VAUGHAN

They Are All Gone into the World of Light

They are all gone into the world of light!
   And I alone sit ling'ring here;
Their very memory is fair and bright,
   And my sad thoughts doth clear.

It glows and glitters in my cloudy breast,
   Like stars upon some gloomy grove,
Or those faint beams in which this hill is dressed,
   After the sun's remove.

I see them walking in an air of glory,
   Whose light doth trample on my days:
My days, which are at best but dull and hoary,
   Mere glimmering and decays.

O holy Hope! and high Humility,
   High as the heavens above!
These are your walks, and you have showed them me,
   To kindle my cold love.

Dear, beauteous Death! the jewel of the just,
   Shining nowhere, but in the dark;
What mysteries do lie beyond thy dust,
   Could man outlook that mark!

He that hath found some fledged bird's nest, may know
    At first sight if the bird be flown;
But what fair well or grove he sings in now,
    That is to him unknown.

And yet, as angels in some brighter dreams
    Call to the soul when man doth sleep,
So some strange thoughts transcend our wonted themes,
    And into glory peep.

If a star were confin'd into a tomb,
    Her captive flames must needs burn there;
But when the hand that locked her up, gives room,
    She'll shine through all the sphere.

O Father of eternal life, and all
    Created glories under Thee!
Resume Thy spirit from this world of thrall
    Into true liberty.

Either disperse these mists, which blot and fill
    My perspective, still, as they pass:
Or else remove me hence unto that hill
    Where I shall need no glass.

BEN JONSON

On My First Sonne

Farewell, thou child of my right hand, and joy;
   My sinne was too much hope of thee, lov'd boy,
Seven yeeres tho'wert lent to me, and I thee pay,
   Exacted by thy fate, on the just day.
O, could I loose all father, now. For why
   Will man lament the state he should envie?
To have so soone scap'd worlds, and fleshes rage,
   And, if no other miserie, yet age?
Rest in soft peace, and, ask'd, say here doth lye
   BEN. JONSON his best piece of *poetrie*.
For whose sake, henceforth, all his vowes be such,
   As what he loves may never like too much.

REVEREND JULIAN BICKERSTETH

Letter to His Mother (from *War Diaries, 1914–18*)

5 July 1917

I was distressed to hear from our Colonel that the man who
came to us under arrest as a deserter six months ago and
who had deserted again *four times* since, had been condemned to death. The previous sentence of death passed on him
had been commuted and then suspended to give him
another chance, but he deserted again during the Battle of
Arras and so lost his only chance (. . .)

Monday 2nd July I left our HQ in the Line fairly early and
went straight down to see the Senior Chaplain, who himself
had intended to take on this sad business, but as I have been
seeing the man practically every day for three or four
months I asked him to let me see it through. I felt it was my
duty. So after some lunch with him I went to our Transport
Lines and saw the firing party, picked by military require-
ments from our own men. These men had been sent down
specially from the trenches. I made several arrangements
about the digging of the grave and then went on to the spot
where the promulgation was to take place. This consisted of
the prisoner being marched under escort to a spot just
outside the village. Here he was placed in the centre of a
hollow square formed by representatives drawn from each
battalion in the Brigade. At a given signal the prisoner is
ordered to take two paces to the front, which he does, and

103

his cap is taken off, and then the officer in charge of the parade read the sentence which concluded a recital of the crime for which the prisoner had been found guilty. I stood close behind the prisoner to support him by my presence all I could. There was a terrible silence when the promulgation concluded with the sentence of death. The man seemed a bit dazed, but stepped back to between his guards fairly smartly. I walked off the ground with him. He was taken to a little back room on the second storey of a two-storied semi-detached villa in the village (. . .)

The room was furnished with a small round table, three chairs, and a wire bed raised six inches from the ground. I took a chair and sat next to him. 'I am going to stay with you and do anything I can for you. If you'd like to talk, we will, but if you would rather not, we'll sit quiet.' Two fully armed sentries with fixed bayonets stand one by the door and the other by the window. The room is only nine feet by ten feet. Anything in the nature of a private talk seems likely to be difficult. An appeal that the sentries may be removed is not accepted. There are two bars to the windows and the prisoner might seek to make an end of himself. So I sit on silently. Suddenly I hear great heaving sobs and the prisoner breaks down and cries. In a second I lean over close to him, as he hides his face in his hands, and in a low voice I talk to him. He seems still a little doubtful about his fate and I have to explain to him what is going to happen tomorrow morning. I tell him about Morris and of how many splendid men have 'passed on'. What fine company he will find on the other side. After a time he quietens down and his tea comes up – two large pieces of bread and butter, a mess tin half full of tea and some jam in a tin. One of the sentries lends me his clasp knife, so that I may put jam on his bread, for the prisoner of course is not allowed to handle a knife. After his tea is over, I hand him a pipe and tobacco. These comforts, strictly forbidden to all prisoners, are not with-held now. He loved a pipe and soon he is contentedly puffing away. Time goes on. I know that he must sleep, if possible, during the hours of darkness, so my time is short. How can I reach his soul? I get out my Bible and read to him something from the Gospel. It leaves him unmoved. He is obviously uninterested and my attempt to talk a little about what I have read leaves him cold. Where is my point of contact? I make him move his chair as far away from the sentry as possible, and speaking in a low voice close to him, I am not overheard, but of what to speak? There is no point of contact through his home, which means nothing to him. I get out an army prayerbook, which contains at the end about 130 hymns, and handing him the book, ask him to read through the part at the end, so that, if he can find a hymn he knows, I can read it to him. He hits on 'Rock of Ages' and asks, not if I will read it to him, but if we can sing it. The idea of our solemnly singing hymns together, while the two sentries eye us coldly from the other side of the room, seems to me so incongruous that I put him off with the promise of a hymn to be sung before he goes to sleep, but he is not satisfied and he returns to the suggestion again. This time I had enough sense, thank goodness, to seize on 'the straw', *and we sat there and sang hymns together for three hours or more.*

And the curious thing about this extraordinary man is that he takes command of the proceedings. He chooses the hymns. He will not sing any one over twice. He starts the hymn on the right note, knows the tunes and pitches them all perfectly right. Music has evidently not been denied him. The words mean nothing to him, or else he is so little gifted with imagination that the pathos of such lines as 'Hold Thou Thy cross before my closing eyes' and many similar lines, which in view of the morrow should cut deep, leave the prisoner unmoved.

Oh! how we sang – hymn after hymn. He knew more tunes than I did. Girdlestone came and fetched me away for half an hour's dinner and then I returned to the little room and in the rapidly fading light went on with the hymn-singing. I brought him a YMCA hymn-book, which contained several hymns not in the other. He was delighted and we sang

'Throw out the Lifeline', 'What a Friend we have in Jesus' and others. When 10.30 p.m. came I was anxious to see the prisoner sleeping, for his own sake, though I was willing to go on singing hymns if he wanted to. His stock, however, was nearly exhausted, as he would never sing the same hymn twice over. So we agreed to close the singing, but we would sing one of the hymns he had already sung, a second time as a last effort. So he chose 'God be with us till we meet again'. He sang it utterly unmoved. While I was ruminating over how to make use of the hymns for getting a little further on, he said 'We haven't finished yet – we must have "God save the King"' and we then and there rose to our feet, and the two Divisional Military Police, who had replaced the ordinary guard and been accommodated with two chairs, had to get up and stand rigidly to attention, while the prisoner and I sang lustily three verses of the National Anthem! A few seconds later the prisoner was asleep.

I felt that the hymns, even if the words had not meant much to him, had been a prayer – or rather many prayers – and seeing him inclined to sleep, I did not try to get his attention to pray more with him. I have never spent a stranger evening. I think it was a distinct effort on his part to give Religion full play. To him, hymn-singing meant Religion. Probably no other aspect or side of Religion had ever touched him and now that he was 'up against it' he found real consolation in singing hymns learnt in childhood – he had been to Sunday School up till twelve or thirteen. Anyhow, that was the point of contact I had been seeking for. *All night I sat by his side.* One sentry played patience – the other read a book. Once or twice the prisoner woke up, but he soon slept again. At 3.00 a.m. I watched the first beginnings of dawn through the window. At 3.30 a.m I heard the tramp tramp of the Firing Party marching down the road. A few minutes later the police Sergeant-Major brought me up a cup of tea and I had a whispered consultation with him as to how long I could let the prisoner sleep. A minute or two later I was called down to see the

APM, the divisional officer in charge of the police, and he gave me some rum to give the prisoner if he wanted it. It was a dark morning, so he did not want the prisoner awakened for another ten minutes. I went up again and at the right time wakened him. While his breakfast was being brought up, we knelt together in prayer. I commended him to God and we said together the Lord's Prayer, which he knew quite well and was proud of knowing. Then he sat down and ate a really good breakfast – bread and butter, ham, and tea. When he had finished it was just four o'clock and I poured into his empty mug a tablespoonful of rum, but when he had tasted it, he wouldn't drink any of it. 'Is it time to go?' he said. '*Yes, it is time. I will stay close to you.*' Down the narrow stairs we went and through the silent streets of the village our weird little procession tramped. First a burly military policeman, then the prisoner, un-bound, and myself, followed close on our heels by two more policemen, the APM, the Doctor, and one other officer. We had about 300 yards to go to a deserted and ruined house just outside the village. I held the prisoner's arm tight for sympathy's sake. Reaching the house, the police immediately handcuffed the man and the Doctor blindfolded him. He was breathing heavily and his heart going very quickly, but outwardly he was unmoved. I said a short prayer and led him the ten or twelve paces out into the yard where he was at once bound to a stake. I whispered in his ear 'Safe in the arms of Jesus,' and he repeated quite clearly 'Safe in the arms of Jesus.' The APM motioned me away. In three or four seconds the Firing Party had done their work. Poor lads – I was sorry for them. They felt it a good deal and I followed them out of the yard at once and spoke to them and handed them cigarettes.

Girdlestone turned up and together we took the body in a motor ambulance to the nearest cemetery, where I had a burial party waiting, and *we gave his body Christian burial.*

I went back to the Transport Lines and tried to get some sleep.

EMILY BRONTË

Cold in the Earth

Cold in the earth and the deep snow piled above thee!
Far, far removed, cold in the dreary grave!
Have I forgot, my Only Love, to love thee,
Severed at last by Time's all-wearing wave?

Now, when alone, do my thoughts no longer hover
Over the mountains on Angora's shore;
Resting their wings where heath and fern-leaves cover
That noble heart for ever, ever more?

Cold in the earth, and fifteen wild Decembers
From those brown hills have melted into spring –
Faithful indeed is the spirit that remembers
After such years of change and suffering!

Sweet Love of youth, forgive if I forget thee
While the World's tide is bearing me along:
Sterner desires and darker hopes beset me,
Hopes which obscure but cannot do thee wrong.

No other Sun has lightened up my heaven;
No other Star has ever shone for me:
All my life's bliss from thy dear life was given –
All my life's bliss is in the grave with thee.

But when the days of golden dreams had perished
And even Despair was powerless to destroy,
Then did I learn how existence could be cherished,
Strengthened and fed without the aid of joy.

Then did I check the tears of useless passion,
Weaned my young soul from yearning after thine;
Sternly denied its burning wish to hasten
Down to that tomb already more than mine!

And even yet, I dare not let it languish,
Dare not indulge in Memory's rapturous pain:
Once drinking deep of that divinest anguish,
How could I seek the empty world again?

THE YOUNGER PLINY

Letter 16, from Book 6

To Cornelius Tacitus

Thank you for asking me to send you a description of my uncle's death so that you can leave an accurate account of it for posterity; I know that immortal fame awaits him if his death is recorded by you. It is true that he perished in a catastrophe which destroyed the loveliest regions of the earth, a fate shared by whole cities and their people, and one so memorable that it is likely to make his name live for ever: and he himself wrote a number of books of lasting value: but you write for all time and can still do much to perpetuate his memory. The fortunate man, in my opinion, is he to whom the gods have granted the power either to do something which is worth recording or to write what is worth reading, and most fortunate of all is the man who can do both. Such a man was my uncle, as his own books and yours will prove. So you set me a task I would choose for myself, and I am more than willing to start on it.

My uncle was stationed at Misenum, in active command of the fleet. On 24 August, in the early afternoon, my mother drew his attention to a cloud of unusual size and appearance. He had been out in the sun, had taken a cold bath, and lunched while lying down, and was then working at his books. He called for his shoes and climbed up to a place which would give him the best view of the phenomenon. It was not clear at that distance from which mountain

110

the cloud was rising (it was afterwards known to be Vesuvius); its general appearance can best be expressed as being like an umbrella pine, for it rose to a great height on a sort of trunk and then split off into branches, I imagine because it was thrust upwards by the first blast and then left unsupported as the pressure subsided, or else it was borne down by its own weight so that it spread out and gradually dispersed. In places it looked white, elsewhere blotched and dirty, according to the amount of soil and ashes it carried with it. My uncle's scholarly acumen saw at once that it was important enough for a closer inspection, and he ordered a boat to be made ready, telling me I could come with him if I wished. I replied that I preferred to go on with my studies, and as it happened he had himself given me some writing to do.

As he was leaving the house he was handed a message from Rectina, wife of Tascus whose house was at the foot of the mountain, so that escape was impossible except by boat. She was terrified by the danger threatening her and implored him to rescue her from her fate. He changed his plans, and what he had begun in a spirit of inquiry he completed as a hero. He gave orders for the warships to be launched and went on board himself with the intention of bringing help to many more people besides Rectina, for this lovely stretch of coast was thickly populated. He hurried to the place which everyone else was hastily leaving, steering his course straight for the danger zone. He was entirely fearless, describing each new movement and phase of the portent to be noted down exactly as he observed them. Ashes were already falling, hotter and thicker as the ships drew near, followed by bits of pumice and blackened stones, charred and cracked by the flames: then suddenly they were in shallow water, and the shore was blocked by the debris from the mountain. For a moment my uncle wondered whether to turn back, but when the helmsman advised this he refused, telling him that Fortune stood by the courageous and they must make for Pomponianus at Stabiae. He was cut off there by the breadth of the bay (for the shore

111

gradually curves round a basin filled by the sea); so that he was not as yet in danger, though it was clear that this would come nearer as it spread. Pomponianus had therefore already put his belongings on board ship, intending to escape if the contrary wind fell. This wind was of course full in my uncle's favour, and he was able to bring his ship in. He embraced his terrified friend, cheered and encouraged him, and thinking he could calm his fears by showing his own composure, gave orders that he was to be carried to the bathroom. After his bath he lay down and dined; he was quite cheerful, or at any rate he pretended he was, which was no less courageous.

Meanwhile on Mount Vesuvius broad sheets of fire and leaping flames blazed at several points, their bright glare emphasised by the darkness of night. My uncle tried to allay the fears of his companions by repeatedly declaring that these were nothing but bonfires left by the peasants in their terror, or else empty houses on fire in the districts they had abandoned. Then he went to rest and certainly slept, for as he was a stout man his breathing was rather loud and heavy and could be heard by people coming and going outside his door. By this time the courtyard giving access to his room was full of ashes mixed with pumice-stones, so that its level had risen, and if he had stayed in the room any longer he would never have got out. He was wakened, came out and joined Pomponianus and the rest of the household who had sat up all night. They debated whether to stay indoors or take their chance in the open, for the buildings were now shaking with violent shocks, and seemed to be swaying to and fro as if they were torn from their foundations. Outside on the other hand, there was the danger of falling pumice-stones, even though these were light and porous; however, after comparing the risks they chose the latter. In my uncle's case one reason outweighed the other, but for the others it was a choice of fears. As a protection against falling objects they put pillows on their heads tied down with cloths.

Elsewhere there was daylight by this time, but they were still in darkness, blacker and denser than any ordinary night, which they relieved by lighting torches and various kinds of lamp. My uncle decided to go down to the shore and investigate on the spot the possibility of any escape by sea, but he found the waves still wild and dangerous. A sheet was spread on the ground for him to lie down, and he repeatedly asked for cold water to drink. Then the flames and smell of sulphur which gave warning of the approaching fire drove the others to take flight and roused him to stand up. He stood leaning on two slaves and then suddenly collapsed, I imagine because the dense fumes choked his breathing by blocking his windpipe which was constitutionally weak and narrow and often inflamed. When daylight returned on the 26th – two days after the last day he had seen – his body was found intact and uninjured, still fully clothed and looking more like sleep than death.

Meanwhile my mother and I were at Misenum, but this is not of any historic interest, and you only wanted to hear about my uncle's death. I will say no more, except to add that I have described in detail every incident which I either witnessed myself or heard about immediately after the event, when reports were most likely to be accurate. It is for you to select what best suits your purpose, for there is a great difference between a letter to a friend and history written for all to read.

NORMAN MacCAIG

Praise of a Collie

She was a small dog, neat and fluid –
Even her conversation was tiny:
She greeted you with *bow*, never *bow-wow*.

Her sons stood monumentally over her
But did what she told them. Each grew grizzled
Till it seemed he was his own mother's grandfather.

Once, gathering sheep on a showery day,
I remarked how dry she was. Pollóchan said, 'Ah,
It would take a very accurate drop to hit Lassie.'

She sailed in the dinghy like a proper sea-dog.
Where's a burn? – she's first on the other side.
She flowed through fences like a piece of black wind.

But suddenly she was old and sick and crippled . . .
I grieved for Pollóchan when he took her a stroll
And put his gun to the back of her head.

GEORGE MATHESON

O Love that Wilt Not Let Me Go

O Love that wilt not let me go,
   I rest my weary soul in Thee:
I give Thee back the life I owe,
That in thine ocean depths its flow
     May richer, fuller be.

O Light that followest all my way,
   I yield my flickering torch to Thee:
My heart restores its borrowed ray,
That in Thy sunshine's blaze its day
     May brighter, fairer be.

O Joy that seekest me through pain,
   I cannot close my heart to thee:
I trace the rainbow through the rain,
And feel the promise is not vain,
     That morn shall tearless be.

O Cross that liftest up my head,
   I dare not ask to fly from Thee:
I lay in dust life's glory dead.
And from the ground there blossoms red,
     Life that shall endless be.

ALFRED, LORD TENNYSON

Crossing the Bar

Sunset and evening star,
    And one clear call for me!
And may there be no moaning of the bar,
    When I put out to sea.

But such a tide as moving seems asleep,
    Too full for sound and foam,
When that which drew from out the boundless deep
    Turns again home.

Twilight and evening bell,
    And after that the dark!
And may there be no sadness of farewell,
    When I embark;

For though from out our bourne of Time and Place
    The flood may bear me far,
I hope to see my Pilot face to face
    When I have crossed the bar.

PHILIP LARKIN

Aubade

I work all day, and get half-drunk at night.
Waking at four to soundless dark, I stare.
In time the curtain-edges will grow light.
Till then I see what's really always there:
Unresting death, a whole day nearer now,
Making all thought impossible but how
And where and when I shall myself die.
Arid interrogation: yet the dread
Of dying, and being dead,
Flashes afresh to hold and horrify.

The mind blanks at the glare. Not in remorse
– The good not done, the love not given, time
Torn off unused – nor wretchedly because
An only life can take so long to climb
Clear of its wrong beginnings, and may never;
But at the total emptiness for ever,
The sure extinction that we travel to
And shall be lost in always. Not to be here,
Not to be anywhere,
And soon; nothing more terrible, nothing more true.

This is a special way of being afraid
No trick dispels. Religion used to try,
That vast moth-eaten musical brocade
Created to pretend we never die,

And specious stuff that says *No rational being*
Can fear a thing it will not feel, not seeing
That this is what we fear – no sight, no sound,
No touch or taste or smell, nothing to think with,
Nothing to love or link with,
The anaesthetic from which none come round.

And so it stays just on the edge of vision,
A small unfocused blur, a standing chill
That slows each impulse down to indecision.
Most things may never happen: this one will,
And realisation of it rages out
In furnace-fear when we are caught without
People or drink. Courage is no good:
It means not scaring others. Being brave
Lets no one off the grave.
Death is no different whined at than withstood.

Slowly light strengthens, and the room takes shape.
It stands plain as a wardrobe, what we know,
Have always known, know that we can't escape,
Yet can't accept. One side will have to go.
Meanwhile telephones crouch, getting ready to ring
In locked-up offices, and all the uncaring
Intricate rented world begins to rouse.
The sky is white as clay, with no sun.
Work has to be done.
Postmen like doctors go from house to house.

GERARD MANLEY HOPKINS

Spring and Fall: To a Young Child

Márgarét, áre you grieving
Over Goldengrove unleaving?
Leáves, like the things of man, you
With your fresh thoughts care for, can you?
Ah! ás the heart grows older
It will come to such sights colder
By and by, nor spare a sigh
Though worlds of wanwood leafmeal lie;
And yet you will weep and know why.
Now no matter, child, the name:
Sórrow's spríngs áre the same.
Nor mouth had, no nor mind, expressed
What heart heard of, ghost guessed:

It is the blight man was born for,
It is Margaret you mourn for.

WILLIAM SHAKESPEARE

from *King John*

Grief fills the room up of my absent child,
Lies in his bed, walks up and down with me,
Puts on his pretty looks, repeats his words,
Remembers me of all his gracious parts,
Stuffs out his vacant garments with his form:
Then have I reason to be fond of grief.

OVID

The Last Night in Rome

When I recall the most sad picture of that night, the last moments I had in Rome, when I remember the night I left so much that is dear to me, even now a tear falls from my eyes. Already the morning had almost come on which Caesar had bidden me leave the frontiers of Italy. I had neither the time nor the heart to get ready: my mind had grown numb with the long delay. I could not bother with servants or choosing companions or with the clothes or money that an exile should have. I was bewildered like someone who is struck by Jove's lightning and still lives and is unconscious of living. But when my very grief drove this cloud from my mind, and at last my senses rallied, before I went I talked for the last time to my sad friends, just the one or two out of many, who remained. My loving wife embraced me, her own tears more bitter than mine, as their shower kept falling down her guiltless cheeks. My daughter was far away in other parts, on the coast of Libya, and could not be told of my fate. Wherever you looked, there was the sound of grief and groans, and indoors it seemed like the wailing of a funeral. Men and women, and slaves too, were mourning at my passing and every corner in the house had its tears. If in a small matter I may use a great example, this was the look Troy had, when it was captured.

WILLIAM WORDSWORTH

from *Ode: Intimations of Immortality from Recollections of Early Childhood*

The Child is father of the Man;
And I could wish my days to be
Bound each to each by natural piety.

There was a time when meadow, grove, and stream,
The earth, and every common sight,
    To me did seem
  Apparelled in celestial light,
The glory and the freshness of a dream.
It is not now as it hath been of yore; –
   Turn wheresoe'er I may,
    By night or day,
The things which I have seen I now can see no more.

   The Rainbow comes and goes,
   And lovely is the Rose,
   The Moon doth with delight
Look round her when the heavens are bare,
   Waters on a starry night
   Are beautiful and fair;
The sunshine is a glorious birth;
But yet I know, where'er I go.
That there hath past away a glory from the earth.
. . .

Ye blessèd Creatures, I have heard the call
    Ye to each other make; I see
The heavens laugh with you in your jubilee;
    My heart is at your festival,
        My head hath its coronal,
The fulness of your bliss, I feel – I feel it all.
        Oh evil day! if I were sullen
        While Earth herself is adorning,
            This sweet May-morning,
        And the Children are culling
            On every side,
    In a thousand valleys far and wide,
    Fresh flowers; while the sun shines warm,
And the Babe leaps up on his Mother's arm: –
    I hear, I hear, with joy I hear!
    – But there's a Tree, of many, one,
A single Field which I have looked upon,
Both of them speak of something that is gone:
        The Pansy at my feet
        Doth the same tale repeat:
Whither is fled the visionary gleam?
Where is it now, the glory and the dream?

Our birth is but a sleep and a forgetting:
The Soul that rises with us, our life's Star,
    Hath had elsewhere its setting,
        And cometh from afar:
    Not in entire forgetfulness,
    And not in utter nakedness,
But trailing clouds of glory do we come
    From God, who is our home:
Heaven lies about us in our infancy!
Shades of the prison-house begin to close
    Upon the growing Boy,
But He beholds the light, and whence it flows,
    He sees it in his joy;

The Youth, who daily farther from the east
    Must travel, still is Nature's Priest,
    And by the vision splendid
    Is on his way attended;
At length the Man perceives it die away,
And fade into the light of common day.

ELIZABETH JENNINGS

One Flesh

Lying apart now, each in a separate bed,
He with a book, keeping the light on late,
She like a girl dreaming of childhood,
All men elsewhere – it is as if they wait
Some new event: the book he holds unread,
Her eyes fixed on the shadows overhead.

Tossed up like flotsam from a former passion,
How cool they lie. They hardly ever touch,
Or if they do it is like a confession
Of having little feeling – or too much.
Chastity faces them, a destination
For which their whole lives were a preparation.

Strangely apart, yet strangely close together,
Silence between them like a thread to hold
And not wind in. And time itself's a feather
Touching them gently. Do they know they're old,
These two who are my father and my mother
Whose fire from which I came, has now grown cold?

ELIZABETH SMART

from *By Grand Central Station I Sat Down And Wept*

Is it possible he cannot hear me when he lies so close, so lightly asleep? These hours are the only hours. What can sleep give him to compare with what I could have given him? He must start up. He must come here and find me.

He cries out in his sleep. He sees the huge bird of catastrophe fly by. Both its wings are lined with the daily paper. Five million other voices are shrieking too. How shall I be heard?

'Lie still, my dear,' his guardian angel says.

'Is everything all right?'

'No, but lie still all the same.'

Dawn creeps over his window like a guilty animal. This is the very room he chose instead of love. Let it be quiet and full of healing. For me it blocks all vision, all perspective. It is the cursed comfort he preferred to my breast.

The one who shares it weeps silently in corners, is tender unnoticed, and makes his necessary tea.

'Have you seen my notebook, dear?'

'It is under the desk, my sweet.'

Give it to him, O my gentle usurper, whom I also have usurped, my enemy whom I have both killed and been killed by. Let him write words that will acquit him of these murders.

The page is as white as my face after a night of weeping. It

126

is as sterile as my devastated mind. All martyrdoms are in vain. He also is drowning in the blood of too much sacrifice.

Lay aside the weapons, love, for all battles are lost.

W.H. AUDEN

Dear, Though the Night Is Gone

Dear, though the night is gone,
The dream still haunts today
That brought us to a room,
Cavernous, lofty as
A railway terminus,
And crowded in that gloom
Were beds, and we in one
In a far corner lay.

Our whisper woke no clocks,
We kissed and I was glad
At everything you did,
Indifferent to those
Who sat with hostile eyes
In pairs on every bed,
Arms round each other's necks,
Inert and vaguely sad.

O but what worm of guilt
Or what malignant doubt
Am I the victim of;
That you then, unabashed,
Did what I never wished,
Confessed another love;
And I, submissive, felt
Unwanted and went out?

MICHAEL DRAYTON

Since There's No Help, Come Let Us Kiss and Part

Since there's no help, come let us kiss and part;
Nay, I have done, you get no more of me,
And I am glad, yea, glad with all my heart
That thus so cleanly I myself can free;
Shake hands for ever, cancel all our vows,
And when we meet at any time again,
Be it not seen in either of our brows
That we one jot of former love retain.
Now at the last gasp of Love's latest breath,
When, his pulse failing, Passion speechless lies,
When Faith is kneeling by his bed of death,
And Innocence is closing up his eyes,
    Now if thou wouldst, when all have given him over,
    From death to life thou mightst him yet recover.

CAROL ANN DUFFY

Mean Time

The clocks slid back an hour
and stole light from my life
as I walked through the wrong part of town,
mourning our love.

And, of course, unmendable rain
fell to the bleak streets
where I felt my heart gnaw
at all our mistakes.

If the darkening sky could lift
more than one hour from this day
there are words I would never have said
nor have heard you say.

But we will be dead, as we know,
beyond all light.
These are the shortened days
and the endless nights.

ALBERT CAMUS

from *The Outsider*

As I was being taken from the courthouse to the prison van, I was conscious for a few brief moments of the once familiar feel of a summer evening out of doors. And, sitting in the darkness of my moving cell, I recognised, echoing in my tired brain, all the characteristic sounds of a town I'd loved, and of a certain hour of the day which I had always particularly enjoyed. The shouts of newspaper-boys in the already languid air, the last calls of birds in the public garden, the cries of sandwich-vendors, the screech of trams at the steep corners of the upper town, and that faint rustling overhead as darkness sifted down upon the harbour – all these sounds made my return to prison like a blind man's journey along a route whose every inch he knows by heart.

Yes, this was the evening hour when – how long ago it seemed! – I always felt so well content with life. Then, what awaited me was a night of easy, dreamless sleep. This was the same hour, but with a difference; I was returning to a cell and what awaited me was a night haunted by forebodings of the coming day. And so I learnt that familiar paths traced in the dusk of summer evenings may lead as well to prison as to innocent, carefree sleep.

GERARD MANLEY HOPKINS

'I wake and feel the fell of dark, not day'

I wake and feel the fell of dark, not day.
What hours, O what black hoürs we have spent
This night! what sights you, heart, saw; ways you went!
And more must, in yet longer light's delay.
  With witness I speak this. But where I say
Hours I mean years, mean life. And my lament
Is cries countless, cries like dead letters sent
To dearest him that lives alas! away.

  I am gall, I am heartburn. God's most deep decree
Bitter would have me taste: my taste was me;
Bones built in me, flesh filled, blood brimmed the curse.
  Selfyeast of spirit a dull dough sours. I see
The lost are like this, and their scourge to be
As I am mine, their sweating selves; but worse.

WILLIAM SHAKESPEARE

Sigh No More

Sigh no more Ladies, sigh no more
Men were deceivers ever,
One foote in Sea, and one on shore,
To one thing constant never,
Then sigh not so, but let them goe,
And be you blithe and bonnie,
Converting all your sounds of woe,
Into hey nony nony.

Sing no more ditties, sing no moe,
Of dumps so dull and heavy,
The fraud of men were ever so,
Since summer first was leavy,
Then sigh not so, but let them goe,
And be you blithe and bonny,
Converting all your sounds of woe,
Into hey nony nony.

ALFRED, LORD TENNYSON

Mariana

('Mariana in the moated grange' – *Measure for Measure*)

With blackest moss the flower-plots
    Were thickly crusted, one and all:
The rusted nails fell from the knots
    That held the peach to the garden-wall.
The broken sheds looked sad and strange:
    Unlifted was the clinking latch;
    Weeded and worn the ancient thatch
Upon the lonely moated grange.
        She only said, 'My life is dreary,
           He cometh not,' she said;
        She said, 'I am aweary, aweary.
           I would that I were dead!'

Her tears fell with the dews at even;
    Her tears fell ere the dews were dried;
She could not look on the sweet heaven,
    Either at morn or eventide.
After the flitting of the bats,
    When thickest dark did trance the sky,
    She drew her casement-curtain by,
And glanced athwart the glooming flats.
        She only said, 'The night is dreary,
           He cometh not,' she said;

She said, 'I am aweary, aweary,
    I would that I were dead!'

Upon the middle of the night,
    Waking she heard the night-fowl crow:
The cock sung out an hour ere light:
    From the dark fen the oxen's low
Came to her: without hope of change,
    In sleep she seemed to walk forlorn,
    Till cold winds woke the grey-eyed morn
About the lonely moated grange.
    She only said, 'The day is dreary,
      He cometh not,' she said;
    She said, 'I am aweary, aweary,
      I would that I were dead!'

About a stone-cast from the wall
    A sluice with blackened waters slept,
And o'er it many, round and small,
    The clustered marish-mosses crept.
Hard by a poplar shook alway,
    All silver-green with gnarlèd bark:
    For leagues no other tree did mark
The level waste, the rounding grey.
    She only said, 'My life is dreary,
      He cometh not,' she said;
    She said, 'I am aweary, aweary,
      I would that I were dead!'

And ever when the moon was low.
    And the shrill winds were up and away,
In the white curtain, to and fro,
    She saw the gusty shadow sway.
But when the moon was very low,
    And wild winds bound within their cell,
    The shadow of the poplar fell
Upon her bed, across her brow.

She only said, 'The night is dreary,
  He cometh not,' she said;
She said, 'I am aweary, aweary,
  I would that I were dead!'

All day within the dreamy house,
  The doors upon their hinges creaked;
The blue fly sung in the pane: the mouse
  Behind the mouldering wainscot shrieked,
Or from the crevice peered about.
  Old faces glimmered thro' the doors,
  Old footsteps trod the upper floors,
Old voices called her from without.
  She only said, 'My life is dreary,
    He cometh not,' she said;
  She said, 'I am aweary, aweary,
    I would that I were dead!'

R.D. LAING

from *The Politics of Experience*

*As a medical student, Laing attended the delivery
of a child:*

Finally it started to come – grey, slimy, cold – out it came –
a large human frog – an anencephalic monster, no neck, no
head, with eyes, nose, froggy mouth, long arms. This
creature was born at 9.10 a.m. on a clear August morning.
Maybe it was slightly alive. We didn't want to know. We
wrapped it in newspaper – and with this bundle under my
arm to take back to the pathology lab, that seemed to cry
out for all the answerable answers that I ever asked, I
walked along O'Connell Street two hours later. I needed a
drink. I went into a pub, put a bundle on the bar. Suddenly
the desire, to unwrap it, hold it up for all to see, a ghastly
Gorgon's head, to turn the world to stone.

LAURENCE BINYON

For the Fallen

With proud thanksgiving, a mother for her children,
England mourns for her dead across the sea.
Flesh of her flesh they were, spirit of her spirit,
Fallen in the cause of the free.

Solemn the drums thrill: Death august and royal
Sings sorrow up into immortal spheres.
There is music in the midst of desolation
And a glory that shines upon our tears.

They went with songs to the battle, they were young,
Straight of limb, true of eye, steady and aglow.
They were staunch to the end against odds uncounted,
They fell with their faces to the foe.

They shall grow not old, as we that are left grow old:
Age shall not weary them, nor the years condemn.
At the going down of the sun and in the morning
We will remember them.

They mingle not with their laughing comrades again;
They sit no more at familiar tables of home;
They have no lot in our labour of the day-time;
They sleep beyond England's foam.

But where our desires are and our hopes profound,
Felt as a well-spring that is hidden from sight,
To the innermost heart of their own land they are known
As the stars are known to the Night;

As the stars that shall be bright when we are dust,
Moving in marches upon the heavenly plain,
As the stars that are starry in the time of our darkness,
To the end, to the end, they remain.

SIR WALTER RALEGH

Even Such Is Time
(written on the eve of his execution)

Even such is time that takes in trust
Our youth, our joys, our all we have,
And pays us but with age and dust,
Who in the dark and silent grave,
When we have wandered all our ways,
Shuts up the story of our days.
But from this earth, this grave, this dust,
My God shall raise me up, I trust.

EDWIN MUIR

from 'Variations on a Time Theme'

Lost love that flies aghast
It knows not where
And finds no foothold
But the dreadful air.

THE BIBLE

By the Rivers of Babylon (Psalm 137)

By the rivers of Babylon, there we sat down, yea, we wept, when we remembered Zion.

We hanged our harps upon the willows in the midst thereof.

For there they that carried us away captive required of us a song, and they that wasted us *required of us* mirth, *saying*, Sing us *one* of the songs of Zion.

How shall we sing the LORD's song in a strange land?

If I forget thee, O Jerusalem, let my right hand forget *her cunning.*

If I do not remember thee, let my tongue cleave to the roof of my mouth; if I prefer not Jerusalem above my chief joy.

Remember, O LORD, the children of Edom in the day of Jerusalem; who said, Rase *it*, rase *it*, *even* to the foundation thereof.

O daughter of Babylon, who art to be destroyed; happy *shall he be*, that rewardeth thee as thou hast served us.

Happy *shall he be*, that taketh and dasheth thy little ones against the stones.

CHIDIOCK TICHBORNE

Elegy, Written with His Own Hand in the Tower before His Execution

My prime of youth is but a frost of cares,
   My feast of joy is but a dish of pain,
My crop of corn is but a field of tares,
   And all my good is but vain hope of gain:
The day is past, and yet I saw no sun,
And now I live, and now my life is done.

My tale was heard, and yet it was not told,
   My fruit is fall'n, and yet my leaves are green,
My youth is spent, and yet I am not old,
   I saw the world, and yet I was not seen:
My thread is cut, and yet it is not spun,
And now I live, and now my life is done.

I sought my death, and found it in my womb,
   I looked for life, and saw it was a shade,
I trod the earth, and knew it was my tomb,
   And now I die, and now I was but made:
My glass is full, and now my glass is run,
And now I live, and now my life is done.

PHILIP LARKIN

Dublinesque

Down stucco sidestreets,
Where light is pewter
And afternoon mist
Brings lights on in shops
Above race-guides and rosaries,
A funeral passes.

The hearse is ahead,
But after there follows
A troop of streetwalkers
In wide flowered hats,
Leg-of-mutton sleeves,
And ankle-length dresses.

There is an air of great friendliness,
As if they were honouring
One they were fond of;
Some caper a few steps,
Skirts held skilfully
(Someone claps time),

And of great sadness also.
As they wend away
A voice is heard singing

Of Kitty, or Katy,
As if the name meant once
All love, all beauty.

GERARD MANLEY HOPKINS

Binsey Poplars

(felled 1879)

My aspens dear, whose airy cages quelled,
Quelled or quenched in leaves the leaping sun,
All felled, felled, are all felled;
    Of a fresh and following folded rank
              Not spared, not one
              That dandled a sandalled
          Shadow that swam or sank
On meadow and river and wind-wandering weed-winding
    bank.

O if we but knew what we do
        When we delve or hew –
    Hack and rack the growing green!
        Since country is so tender
    To touch, her being só slender,
    That, like this sleek and seeing ball
    But a prick will make no eye at all,
    Where we, even where we mean
           To mend her we end her,
      When we hew or delve:
After-comers cannot guess the beauty been.
    Ten or twelve, only ten or twelve
      Strokes of havoc únselve

The sweet especial scene,
Rural scene, a rural scene.
Sweet especial rural scene.

COLETTE

A Blackbird (from *Earthly Paradise*)

I once saw her hang up a scarecrow in a cherry tree to frighten the blackbirds, because our kindly neighbour of the west, who always had a cold and was shaken with bouts of sneezing, never failed to disguise his cherry trees as old tramps and crown his currant bushes with battered opera hats. A few days later I found my mother beneath the tree, motionless with excitement, her head turned toward the heavens in which she would allow human religions no place.

'Sssh! Look!'

A blackbird, with a green and violet sheen on his dark plumage, was pecking at the cherries, drinking their juice and lacerating their rosy pulp.

'How beautiful he is!' whispered my mother. 'Do you see how he uses his claw? And the movements of his head and that arrogance of his? See how he twists his beak to dig out the stone! And you notice that he only goes for the ripest ones.'

'But, mother, the scarecrow!'

'Sssh! The scarecrow doesn't worry him!'

'But, mother, the cherries!'

My mother brought the glance of her rain-coloured eyes back to earth: 'The cherries? Yes, of course, the cherries.'

In those eyes there flickered a sort of wild gaiety, a contempt for the whole world, a lighthearted disdain which cheerfully spurned me along with everything else. It was only momentary, and it was not the first time I had seen it. Now that I know her better, I can interpret those sudden gleams in her face. They were, I feel, kindled by an urge to escape from everyone and everything, to soar to some high place where only her own writ ran. If I am mistaken, leave me to my delusion.

But there, under the cherry tree, she returned to earth once more among us, weighed down with anxieties, and love, and a husband and children who clung to her. Faced with the common round of life, she became good and comforting and humble again.

'Yes, of course, the cherries . . . you must have cherries too.'

The blackbird, gorged, had flown off, and the scarecrow waggled his empty opera hat in the breeze.

JOHN KEATS

'When I have fears that I may cease to be'

When I have fears that I may cease to be
   Before my pen has glean'd my teeming brain,
Before high-piled books, in charactery,
   Hold like rich garners the full-ripen'd grain;
When I behold, upon the night's starr'd face,
   Huge cloudy symbols of a high romance,
And think that I may never live to trace
   Their shadows, with the magic hand of chance;
And when I feel, fair creature of an hour,
   That I shall never look upon thee more,
Never have relish in the faery power
   Of unreflecting love; – then on the shore
Of the wide world I stand alone, and think,
Till love and fame to nothingness do sink.

RAFFAELLA BARKER

from *Come and Tell Me Some Lies*

There followed the slowest days of my life. Minutes spiralled, never turning into hours as we went through the curious, secret rituals which death brings. Dad died on the day the clocks went back, a day he had always hated for its dismal acceptance of winter. And winter arrived, bringing sharp bright days which faded early, the sky red behind shivering black trees denuded by flint-sharp wind.

Pucker's, the undertakers, bustled into action. They laid Dad out in their breeze-block Chapel of Rest; when empty of death it doubled up as an electrician's workshop. Fearful, but unable to stay away, Poppy, Brodie and I went with Mum to see Dad there. Trussed in white satin frills like a babe prepared for christening, he lay in a silk-lined coffin. I kissed his forehead. He was colder than stone. Brodie cried. Poppy, Mum and I stood dry-eyed, absorbing every detail. I didn't feel he was there. Dad would never wear white frills. He had to be somewhere else, in his fisherman's cap and old suede jacket, laughing at his corpse.

Pucker's telephoned the next morning. They had decided I was in charge, and having asked my name, clung to it.

'Hello, is that Mrs Gabrielly? Pucker's here. We just wondered if you would like the grave dug double deep?'

'What for? I don't know anything about graves.'

'Well, in case you want to pop your Mum in later.' Mrs Pucker's voice was a mixture of brisk practicality and motherly sympathy.

My knees buckled, and I agreed. 'Oh yes. Whatever you think is best. I don't think I'll ask her now though.' I told Mum later, and she doubled up with laughter.

We, her children, hovered around her, trying anything, everything, to protect her from loss, and knowing we could do nothing.

A friend brought six little brown bottles of Rescue Remedy; they were labelled for each of us. 'What's the difference between them?' Dan wondered. He took a drop from each. 'Mum's is neat brandy. Va Va's is water, and mine tastes like Coca-Cola. Who wants to swap?' He was sent outside to gather wood.

Preparing for a funeral is like making party arrangements with a knife in your spine. This, with obituaries and letters from long-ago friends, was like one of Dad's book launches. A hundred times I opened my mouth to say, 'I must show this to Dad,' only to close it foolishly.

The Old Sweet Dove of Wiveton

'Twas the voice of the sweet dove
I heard him move
I heard him cry
Love, love.

High in the chestnut tree
Is the nest of the old dove
And there he sits solitary
Crying, Love, love.

The grey of this heavy day
Makes the green of the trees' leaves and the grass brighter
And the flowers of the chestnut tree whiter
And whiter the flowers of the high cow-parsley.

So still is the air
So heavy the sky
You can hear the splash
Of the water falling from the green grass
As Red and Honey push by,
The old dogs,
Gone away, gone hunting by the marsh bogs.

Happy the retriever dogs in their pursuit
Happy in bog-mud the busy foot.

Now all is silent, it is silent again
In the sombre day and the beginning soft rain
It is a silence made more actual
By the moan from the high tree that is occasional,
Where in his nest above
Still sits the old dove,
Murmuring solitary
Crying for pain,
Crying most melancholy
Again and again.

The Exequy (For His Wife)

Accept, thou shrine of my dead Saint!
Instead of dirges this complaint;
And for sweet flowers to crown thy hearse,
Receive a strew of weeping verse
From thy griev'd friend, whom thou might'st see
Quite melted into tears for thee.
   Dear loss! since thy untimely fate
My task hath been to meditate
On thee, on thee: thou art the book,
The library whereon I look
Though almost blind. For thee (lov'd clay!)
I languish out, not live the day,
Using no other exercise
But what I practise with mine eyes.
By which wet glasses I find out
How lazily time creeps about
To one that mourns: this, only this
My exercise and bus'ness is:
So I compute the weary hours
With sighs dissolved into showers.

   Nor wonder if my time go thus
Backward and most preposterous;
Thou hast benighted me. Thy set
This eve of blackness did beget,

Who wast my day (though overcast
Before thou had'st thy noon-tide passed),
And I remember must in tears,
Thou scarce had'st seen so many years
As day tells hours. By thy clear sun
My love and fortune first did run;
But thou wilt never more appear
Folded within my hemisphere,
Since both thy light and motion
Like a fled star is fall'n and gone;
And 'twixt me and my soul's dear wish
The earth now interposèd is,
Which such a strange eclipse doth make
As ne'er was read in almanake.

   I could allow thee for a time
To darken me and my sad clime,
Were it a month, a year, or ten,
I would thy exile live till then;
And all that space my mirth adjourn
So thou wouldst promise to return;
And putting off thy ashy shroud
At length disperse this sorrow's cloud.

   But woe is me! the longest date
Too narrow is to calculate
These empty hopes. Never shall I
Be so much blest, as to descry
A glimpse of thee, till that day come
Which shall the earth to cinders doom,
And a fierce fever must calcine
The body of this world, like thine
(My little world!). That fit of fire
Once off, our bodies shall aspire
To our souls' bliss: then we shall rise,
And view ourselves with clearer eyes
In that calm region, where no night
Can hide us from each other's sight.

   Meantime, thou hast her earth: much good

May my harm do thee. Since it stood
With Heaven's will I might not call
Her longer mine, I give thee all
My short-liv'd right and interest
In her, whom living I lov'd best:
With a most free and bounteous grief,
I give thee what I could not keep.
Be kind to her, and prithee look
Thou write into thy Doomsday book
Each parcel of this rarity
Which in thy casket shrin'd doth lie:
See that thou make thy reck'ning straight,
And yield her back again by weight;
For thou must audit on thy trust
Each grain and atom of this dust:
As thou wilt answer Him, that lent,
Not gave thee, my dear monument.
   So close the ground, and 'bout her shade
Black curtains draw, my bride is laid.
   Sleep on my love in thy cold bed
Never to be disquieted!
My last good night! Thou wilt not wake
Till I thy fate shall overtake:
Till age, or grief, or sickness must
Marry my body to that dust
It so much loves; and fill the room
My heart keeps empty in thy tomb.
Stay for me there; I will not fail
To meet thee in that hollow vale.
And think not much of my delay;
I am already on the way,
And follow thee with all the speed
Desire can make, or sorrows breed.
Each minute is a short degree
And ev'ry hour a step towards thee.
At night when I betake to rest,
Next morn I rise nearer my west

Of life, almost by eight hours' sail,
Than when sleep breath'd his drowsy gale.
    Thus from the sun my bottom steers,
And my days' compass downward bears.
Nor labour I to stem the tide,
Through which to thee I swiftly glide.
    'Tis true; with shame and grief I yield,
Thou, like the van, first took'st the field,
And gotten hast the victory
In thus adventuring to die
Before me; whose more years might crave
A just precedence in the grave.

But hark! My pulse, like a soft drum
Beats my approach, tells thee I come;
And slow howe'er my marches be,
I shall at last sit down by thee.
    The thought of this bids me go on,
And wait my dissolution
With hope and comfort. Dear! (forgive
The crime) I am content to live
Divided, with but half a heart,
Till we shall meet and never part.

W.B. YEATS

The Choice

The intellect of man is forced to choose
Perfection of the life, or of the work,
And if it take the second must refuse
A heavenly mansion, raging in the dark.
When all that story's finished, what's the news?
In luck or out the toil has left its mark:
That old perplexity an empty purse,
Or the day's vanity, the night's remorse.

W.H. AUDEN

from 'In Memory of W.B. Yeats'

He disappeared in the dead of winter:
The brooks were frozen, the airports almost deserted,
And snow disfigured the public statues;
The mercury sank in the mouth of the dying day.
What instruments we have agree
The day of his death was a dark cold day.

Far from his illness
The wolves ran on through the evergreen forests,
The peasant river was untempted by the fashionable quays;
By mourning tongues
The death of the poet was kept from his poems.

But for him it was his last afternoon as himself,
An afternoon of nurses and rumours;
The provinces of his body revolted,
The squares of his mind were empty,
Silence invaded the suburbs,
The current of his feeling failed; he became his admirers.

Now he is scattered among a hundred cities
And wholly given over to unfamiliar affections,
To find his happiness in another kind of wood
And be punished under a foreign code of conscience.
The words of a dead man
Are modified in the guts of the living.

But in the importance and noise of tomorrow
When the brokers are roaring like beasts on the floor of the
    Bourse,
And the poor have the sufferings to which they are fairly
    accustomed,
And each in the cell of himself is almost convinced of his
    freedom,
A few thousand will think of this day
As one thinks of a day when one did something slightly
    unusual.
What instruments we have agree
The day of his death was a dark cold day.

LAURENCE BINYON

The Burning of the Leaves

Now is the time for the burning of the leaves.
They go to the fire; the nostril pricks with smoke
Wandering slowly into a weeping mist.
Brittle and blotched, ragged and rotten sheaves!
A flame seizes the smouldering ruin and bites
On stubborn stalks that crackle as they resist.

The last hollyhock's fallen tower is dust;
All the spices of June are a bitter reek,
All the extravagant riches spent and mean.
All burns! The reddest rose is a ghost;
Sparks whirl up, to expire in the mist: the wild
Fingers of fire are making corruption clean.

Now is the time for stripping the spirit bare,
Time for the burning of days ended and done,
Idle solace of things that have gone before:
Rootless hopes and fruitless desire are there;
Let them go to the fire, with never a look behind.
The world that was ours is a world that is ours no more.

They will come again, the leaf and the flower, to arise
From squalor of rottenness into the old splendour,
And magical scents to a wondering memory bring;
The same glory, to shine upon different eyes.

Earth cares for her own ruins, naught for ours.
Nothing is certain, only the certain spring.

HORACE

Carpe Diem

Don't ask (we may not know), Leuconoe,
    What the gods plan for you or me.
        Leave the Chaldees to parse
        The sentence of the stars.

Better to bear the outcome, good or bad,
    Whether Jove purposes to add
        Fresh winters to the past
        Or to make this the last

Which now tires out the Tuscan sea and mocks
    Its strength with barricades of rocks.
        Be wise, strain clear the wine
        And prune the rambling vine

Of expectation. Life's short. Even while
    We talk Time, hateful, runs a mile.
        Don't trust tomorrow's bough
        For fruit. Pluck this, here, now.

GEORGE BARKER

A Version of Animula Vagula Blandula

I know where you are now. But do you know?
Are you here in this word? I have not heard
you whistling in the dark. Do not allow
the noun or pronoun or the verb to disturb you.
Sometimes, I think that death is really no joke
but then I have died only two or three such times.
Perhaps there is always someone to attend the
absconding mountebank. But you, farewelling ghost, poor
imperial little thing, go you alone?
Go you alone to the altering? Or am I with you?

PETRONIUS

The Widow of Ephesus (from *Satyrica*)

'There once was a lady of Ephesus who was so famous for
her virtue that women came from foreign countries just to
get a look at her. So when this woman buried her husband,
it wasn't enough for her to grieve in the usual way by
walking behind the corpse with her hair down or by beating
her bare breast before a crowd of mourners; instead she
followed the dead man right into his tomb. She had the
corpse placed in a vault underground, in the Greek fashion,
where she tended it and continued to mourn night and day.
She was so grief-stricken that neither her friends nor her
parents could dissuade her from seeking death by starva-
tion. Finally, even the local magistrates went away, their
pleas rebuffed; everyone had given her up for dead, this
exemplary woman, who had already gone five days without a bite to eat. The poor widow's only company was a
faithful maid, who shared her tears and refilled the lamp in
the tomb as often as it went out. Soon all Ephesus talked of
only one thing; men of every rank agreed: this woman was
the sole true embodiment of wifely love and devotion.

'Meanwhile the provincial governor gave orders that
some thieves be crucified not far from the little tomb where
the widow was mourning the body of her husband. On the
next night a soldier, whose job it was to make sure no one
took one of the criminals down and buried him, noticed a
light flickering among the tombstones and heard the sobs of

someone crying. He was naturally curious to find out who was there and what she was doing. So he walked down into the vault, and the rare beauty of the widow struck him with all the force of an apparition from the underworld. At first he was bewildered, then he noticed the corpse lying there, and the tears and marks of grief on the widow's face, and he understood exactly what he saw: a woman overcome with longing for her dead husband. So he brought his own little supper into the tomb and began to console her; he urged her not to compound her grief with pointless mourning. What good would it do to weep until she broke her heart? Doesn't the same end await us all, the same resting place? And so he reasoned with her using all the arguments that restore sick minds to health.

'But the stranger's attempt to console her only upset her; she tore at her breast more violently, ripped out fistfuls of hair and laid them on the body. Yet the soldier didn't go away. He kept trying to comfort her and give her food; finally, the servant gave in to the scent of the wine and stretched out her hand to his kind offer. Invigorated by food and drink, she began the assault on her mistress' will:

'"What good does it do you to starve to death, to bury yourself alive, to breathe your last breath before the fates demand it?

'"Could ashes or dead souls care less for mourning? Don't you want to live again? Don't you want to shake off this womanish weakness and enjoy the good things of life while you can? Let this corpse lying here be a warning to you – to live!"

'Who can resist it when they're urged to eat or enjoy life? So too the widow, thirsty after days of fasting, lost her resolve and began to fill herself with food no less greedily than the maid who gave in first.

'But you know what appetite remains when our stomachs are full. So the same beguiling arguments that the soldier had used to make the widow want to live, he used again to lay siege to her virtue. Nor did the chaste lady find

167

the young man unpersuasive or uncomely. The maid, too, was trying to win her favour for him and kept saying:

"Will you fight welcome love, as well?"

'Well, why beat around the bush? The woman didn't starve that part of her body either. The persuasive soldier was victorious on both fronts. And they celebrated their marriage not only that night, but the next one as well, and the one after that! (Of course the doors to the tomb were closed!) Indeed, any friend or stranger who came to the tomb would have thought that most virtuous wife had finally expired over the body of her dead husband.

'Well, the soldier took great delight in the widow's beauty and their secret tryst. He kept buying whatever food he could and bringing it to the tomb as soon as night fell. And so it happened that the parents of one of the crucified thieves, seeing there was no one on guard, took their son down one night and gave him the last rites. Tricked while off duty, the next day the soldier discovered that one of the crosses was missing a corpse. Scared to death of being punished, he explained to the widow what had happened. He said he would not wait for a judge to impose a sentence on him, but would punish his negligence with his own sword, if she would kindly make room for a man about to die and use the same fateful tomb for both her lover and her husband!

'But this widow was no less compassionate than she was virtuous! "Heaven forbid that I should have to look upon the bodies of both the men I love at the same time! I would rather sacrifice a dead man than execute a live one!" And she followed her speech with orders that the body of her husband be taken out of his coffin and hung on the empty cross! The soldier adopted this sensible woman's plan, and the next day everyone wondered how a dead man had climbed up on that cross!'

ELAINE FEINSTEIN

Dad

Your old hat hurts me, and those black
    fat raisins you liked to press into
my palm from your soft heavy hand:
    I see you staggering back up the path
with sacks of potatoes from some local farm,
    fresh eggs, flowers. Every day I grieve

for your great heart broken and you gone.
    You loved to watch the trees. This year
you did not see their Spring.
    The sky was freezing over the fen
as on that somewhere secretly appointed day
    you beached: cold, white-faced, shivering.

What happened, old bull, my loyal
    hoarse-voiced warrior? The hammer
blow that stopped you in your track
    and brought you to a hospital monitor
could not destroy your courage
    to the end you were
uncowed and unconcerned with pleasing anyone.

I think of you now as once again safely
    at my mother's side, the earth as
chosen as a bed, and feel most sorrow for

all that was gentle in
my childhood buried there
already forfeit, now forever lost.

WILLIAM SHAKESPEARE

from *Measure for Measure*

Ay, but to die, and go we know not where;
To lie in cold obstruction, and to rot;
This sensible warm motion to become
A kneaded clod; and the delighted spirit
To bathe in fiery floods, or to reside
In thrilling region of thick-ribbed ice.
To be imprison'd in the viewless winds,
And blown with restless violence round about
The pendent world; or to be worse than worst
Of those that lawless and incertain thought
Imagine howling! – 'tis too horrible!
The weariest and most loathed worldly life
That age, ache, penury and imprisonment
Can lay on nature, is a paradise
To what we fear of death.

GEORGE CRABBE

His Late Wife's Wedding-Ring

The ring so worn, as you behold,
So thin, so pale, is yet of gold:
The passion such it was to prove;
Worn with life's cares, love yet was love.

ROBERT BROWNING

Inscription on an Ancient Sundial at Newquay, Cornwall

Sun's light is come: To each
Christ's cross, in shade, doth teach –
'Tis come, thine Hour!
Night brings shade: Going hence
In shade – hear evidence –
'Tis gone, thine Hour!

ACKNOWLEDGEMENTS

The editor and publishers wish to thank the following for permission to use copyright material:

Anvil Press Poetry Ltd for Carol Ann Duffy, 'Mean Time' from *Mean Time* (1993);

Carcanet Press Ltd for Robert Graves, 'Lost Love' from *Collected Poems*; David Wright, 'Et in Arcadia' from *Collected Poems* (1988); and an extract from Helen Thomas, 'World Without End' from Helen Thomas (with Myfanwy Thomas) *Under Storm's Wing* (1997); and Elaine Feinstein, 'Dad' from *Selected Poems*;

Faber and Faber Ltd for George Barker, 'Never, my love and dearest' and 'A Version of Animula Vagula Blandula' from *Collected Poems of George Barker* (1992); W. H. Auden, 'Dear, Though the Night is Gone' and 'Stop all the clocks, cut off the telephone' from 'Twelve Songs' and 'In Memory of W. B. Yeats' from *Collected Poems*; Philip Larkin, 'Dublinesque' and 'Aubade' from *Collected Poems*; William Bell, 'On a Dying Boy' from *Mountains Beneath the Horizon* (1950); and an extract from Sylvia Plath, *The Bell Jar*;

Farrar, Straus & Giroux, Inc for Elizabeth Bishop, 'One Art' from *The Complete Poems 1927–1979.* © 1979, 1983 by Alice Helen Methfessel;

David Higham Associates on behalf of the Estate of the author for Dylan Thomas, 'Do Not Go Gentle Into That Good Night' from *Collected Poems*, J. M. Dent; on behalf of the authors for Elizabeth Jennings, 'One Flesh' from *Collected Poems*, Carcanet; John Heath Stubbs, 'Address Not Known' from *Collected Poems of John Heath Stubbs*, Carcanet (1988); John Pudney, 'For Johnny,' from *The Terrible Rain*, Methuen (1966); and on behalf of the translator for an extract from Horace, 'Carpe Diem', trans. James Michie, Hart Davis (1963);

James MacGibbon for Stevie Smith, 'The Old Sweet Dove of Wiveton', 'Come Death' and 'The Stroke' from *The Collected Poems of Stevie Smith*, Penguin Classics;

John Murray (Publishers) Ltd for John Betjeman, 'Inevitable' from *Collected Poems* (1958);

The Orion Publishing Group Ltd for extracts from Vladimir Nabokov, *Speak, Memory*, Weidenfeld & Nicolson (1969); Petronius, *Satyrica*, trs. R. Bracht Branham and Daniel Kinney, J. M. Dent and Everyman's Library; and with Farrar, Straus & Giroux, Inc. for Robert Pinsky, *The Inferno of Dante: A New Verse Translation*, J. M. Dent. © 1994 by Farrar, Straus & Giroux, Inc., translation © 1994 by Robert Pinsky;

Penguin UK for extracts from Albert Camus, *The First Man*, trans. David Hapgood (1995) Hamish Hamilton, first published by Editions Gallimard, 1994, pp. 18–22. © Editions Gallimard 1994. Trans. © David Hapgood 1995; Albert Camus, *The Outsider*, trans. Stuart Gilbert (1946) Hamish Hamilton, first published as *L'Etranger* by Editions Gallimard, 1942. © Editions Gallimard, 1942. Trans. © Hamish Hamilton 1946; Rafaella Barker, *Come and Tell Me Some Lies*, Hamish Hamilton (1994). © Rafaella Barker 1994; and R. D. Laing, *The Politics of Experience and the Bird of Paradise* (1967) Penguin Books. © R. D. Laing 1967;

Peters Fraser & Dunlop Group Ltd on behalf of the author for an extract from David Wright, *Deafness*, Faber and Faber (1990);

Pen & Sword Books Ltd for an extract from *The Bickersteth Diaries* (1996);